No Shirt. No Shoes....NO PROBLEM!

JEFF FOXWORTHY

No Shirt.
No Shoes....
NO PROBLEM!

HYPERION

New York

LIBRARY OF CONGRESS CATALOGING-IN-PUBLICATION DATA

FOXWORTHY, JEFF.
NO SHIRT. NO SHOES—NO PROBLEM! /
JEFF FOXWORTHY. — 1ST ED.
P.   CM.
ISBN 0-7868-6234-3
1. REDNECK—HUMOR. I. TITLE.
PN6231.R38F675   1996
792′.028′092—dc20
[B]   96-6292
CIP

BOOK DESIGN BY KATHY KIKKERT

FIRST EDITION

1   3   5   7   9   10   8   6   4   2

For my uncle Jack—

a great guy who owns

a mountain of comedy records

and let me listen

to every one of them

To Gregg and the girls

for this and everything else

CONTENTS

SPECIAL THANKS

I don't possess adequate words to thank David Rensin for the talent and effort he brought to this project. Without him, you would be reading a pamphlet, not a book.

When Hyperion approached me, I had just come off tour and had started a television series. I said I simply didn't have the time to write a book and I wasn't sure I had anything to say. Then, I was introduced to David. Because of him, I probably said too much. I knew he was a good writer. I had read his books and Playboy interviews (occasionally even glancing at the pictures). I just didn't know the depth of his skills.

He would meet me at my trailer (work, not home) every day at lunch. He made me talk, he made me think, and we shared a lot of laughs. With his help, I found myself remembering things long forgotten—some of which probably should have stayed that way.

So what you read is my book and his.

Thank you, David.

Jeff Foxworthy

ACKNOWLEDGMENTS

My deepest gratitude to J.P. Williams, Debbie Shaler, Maggie Houlehan, Nina Weinman, Malaika Vereen, Matt Labov, Paul Baker, Amber Gereghty, Mike Smardak, John McDonald, Anne Sibbald, Laurie Abkemeier, Bob Miller, Cynthia Lee Price, CAA, Jay Foxworthy, Mike Higginbotham, and Richard Gudzan.

AUTHOR'S NOTE

Some names have been changed to protect marriages.
I'm still not sure it will help.

No Shirt. No Shoes....NO PROBLEM!

Welcome

I'm not ready to die just yet.

I have my reasons. Can you imagine the floral arrangements? When NASCAR driver Davey Allison was buried in Alabama, *People* magazine ran photos of the flowers at his funeral. There were black carnations in the shape of a race car, a big wheel, and who knows what else. It wouldn't surprise me if someone had made a set of points and plugs out of rose petals.

My wife, Gregg (I call her by her *middle* name), and I were reading in bed at the time. So I showed her the funeral pictures and said, "Since people know me mostly as that *Redneck* guy, I don't even want to *think* about the flowers you'd get if I died now. Rebel flags. Brown carnations shaped like a spit of chewing tobacco juice midflight. Huge bouquets set in tractor tires. And don't forget the wreath that spells out *You might be dead if*... You know I'm proud of my Southern roots, but don't you think I should get a little bit past this Redneck thing before I buy the farm?"

"Does this mean you'll finally stop making jokes about my butt being cold?" she asked. (Because I say onstage that women's rear ends are always cold in bed—and use Gregg's as an example—people stop us on the street and say to her, "So you're the one with the cold butt." She's tired of it.)

"But honey," I said. "That material is *funny*."

Gregg thought for a moment, then said, "Well, I think the worst thing about something bad happening to you—besides the kids and me being alone in this big house with all your stuff, then me having to date again and fall in love . . ."

"Hold on," I interrupted. "I haven't dropped dead *yet*."

". . . would be figuring out what to *do* with all the wonderfully tacky floral arrangements after the funeral," she added, with a reassuring smile.

"Oh, don't worry about that," I said. "You know my family. They'll *beat down* the door to get at those."

Gregg closed her eyes and quickly fell asleep. I didn't. The conversation made me wonder: What was going on in my life that I should have this weird fantasy? Why was I worried about floral arrangements when I should be concerned about more important things such as who would inherit my Ford pickup with the Astro-Turf-lined truck bed. What about the pink plastic flamingos in our front yard? And my collection of stolen road signs?

It took a while before I understood what was bothering me. I felt a kinship with Davey Allison, a regular guy from the South who became a celebrity just doing what he did best. He pursued excellence at his craft and never forgot that he was no different from the people who cheered him on. Flowers in the shape of a race car were just his fans' way of showing their appreciation. Even so, if he'd been standing in the crowd at his own funeral he probably would have felt just like I did at that moment: You never totally adjust to the peculiar things that happen to you when you're famous. Or even semifamous, like me. Of course, I'm not complaining. Success *is* great. But one of my greatest gifts in life is being able to sit with a bunch of guys in a deer-hunting camp just as easily as with Johnny Carson—I'm comfortable in either place. I've always been able to fit in.

That started me thinking about where I'd come from and wondering what had happened to the little boy who grew up three doors down from the end of the old Atlanta airport runway. Believe me, I know I've come a long way. At least now I don't have to pause midsentence every thirty-five seconds to let a plane go overhead. But otherwise, how much is that little boy still a part of me today?

I needed to ponder the changes I'd been through. I ponder on paper; that's how I do my best thinking. The result is this road trip through my life. We'll stop along the way to admire the scenery, answer nature's call, steal a couple of road signs, and tell stories about growing up blue collar, about hunting, fishing, tobacco chewing, girlfriends, love, roommates, sex, work, crazy families, Rednecks, relationships, marriage, kids, comedy, celebrity, holidays, mooning, and a little something I like to call fishball.

I also asked some of my family and friends to add their memories, just to keep me honest. They graciously agreed. Then I changed my mind. It wasn't such a bright idea. They remembered lots of stuff about me that I had *mysteriously* forgotten, and when they reminded me of certain incidents, I suddenly remembered why. But so what if I once rode a pig bareback. And a goat. Just don't ask to see the pictures.

Since you're reading this, I'm assuming that you want to come on in, kick back, and stay awhile. That's fine with me. We're casual here. No shirt? No shoes? No problem! There are no rules to remember, no obligations, no salesman will come to your door. You don't have to kill or skin or gut anything. (The possum hunt comes later and is optional.) The idea is simply to have a good time. If that's not possible, then the idea is to at least get really drunk and think you did.

Either way, I'm hoping that by the time you turn the last page, you'll agree that however strange my life sometimes seems, it's really not so strange after all. Whether you're from North Dallas or North Dakota, I guarantee you'll recognize many funny (okay, unsettling) similarities to your own life, family, and friends. Except for one thing. I'll bet that you've never gotten a gift as weird as the fine home furnishing that Mr. and Mrs. Orville Storch of Sioux City, Iowa, recently sent me. Being who I am and hailing from where I do, I knew with absolute certainty that I was the proud receiver of a wonderful and heartfelt tribute. Imagine: a piece of wood that holds paper plates with the phrase "Redneck China Cabinet" carved crudely across the front.

See, I told you it was too early to die.

Deep Blue
Collar

I grew up so deep blue collar that my mother had to wash my shirts separately, in cold water.

I was born in Atlanta in 1958 and lived in the small suburb of Decatur until I was about six. One of my earliest memories is of getting my head stuck between the porch railing posts. I tried putting my head between the posts to see what would happen—story of my life—and realized pretty quickly that God meant for my ears to bend only in one direction.

My father, Jim Foxworthy, worked for IBM. He's a big man, so we call him Big Jim. Before climbing the management ladder, he just fixed machines. That meant we lived all over the place. From Decatur they transferred him first to Knoxville, Tennessee, and then to Greenville, South Carolina. Along the way, Big Jim and my mom, Carole, had two more kids: my sister, Jennifer, eighteen months younger than me; and my brother Jay, five years younger. We were happy, or so I thought, until I was ten and my parents got divorced.

By the way, their separation didn't scar me for life. I'm not a comedian because I'm still trying to compensate for a bad childhood, being picked on in school, or having a prehensile tail (since removed). My childhood was okay, probably better than many. Divorce just happens, especially in my family. Between my mom and my dad they've been married nine times. As of this writing, they've got Elizabeth Taylor beat by one.

Anyway, we moved in with my mom's folks, James and Mary Camp. They lived on Union Avenue in Hapeville, a small lower-middle-class town eleven miles south of Atlanta.

In Hapeville everybody knew your name. In other words, it was like hanging out at the *Cheers* bar. Such familiarity was mostly comforting, unless, of course, you were a kid who had done something you didn't want your family to find out about. My parents called these informers "good neighbors." We kids just called them snitches.

Hapeville was a great place. It was so small that our morning traffic report depended on a guy looking out his window and saying, "The light is green." Our fire department didn't have a truck, just a long hose. If an emergency happened, you just cupped your hand and yelled "9-1-1!" It was also a safe place. You could ride your bike or walk anywhere with no worries. Our home-security system meant latching the screen door. If our screen was ripped, that was still no cause for alarm. For extra protection we had a No-Pest Strip in the living room.

Our backyard was mostly dirt, but we filled it with interesting stuff like a beat-up basketball backboard and rim through which I could never sink a shot. My mother's family is so tall that nobody ever bothered measuring how high to set the hoop. Standard is ten feet. Ours was more like eleven and a half feet. No wonder in school I was only good at football and baseball.

The backyard also had a pile of concrete blocks, a barrel to burn trash in, and a double kitchen sink turned upside down. My grandfather kept crickets underneath to use as fish bait. My uncles had turned the shack behind the garden into a clubhouse. Inside, they'd hung hardware store posters of women in bikinis holding tools. At the back end of the yard stood a concrete block storage shed. My granddaddy never allowed us inside and never told us why. He guarded that thing. But kids being kids, we eventually picked the lock, snuck in, and poked around. What a disappointment. No beer, no racy magazines, no old hunting dog skeletons. All we found was a garden tiller, fishing gear, a refrigerator stocked with bait, and two huge plastic bags full of rabbits' tails. I think someone should have told Granddaddy that rabbits' *feet* were good luck.

The Hapeville postal service must have figured my family for the stupidest people on the block. Why? My uncle Jimmy one day decided to paint M-A-L-E on our mailbox in big block letters. It was just a joke. We're not idiots. Sometimes I think that living so close to the jet fuel fumes from the planes passing overhead might have had something to do with our odd ways. Every two years the fumes would strip the paint from our cars, so I suppose inhaling the stuff might have affected our brain cells. It certainly would explain the sixth toe on my right foot.

James Camp was Hapeville's assistant fire chief. He didn't have much work, though. Honestly, I don't believe he ever answered a fire alarm. (Once, the high school roof was ablaze, but the firemen couldn't find the school, even though it was just two blocks away. Kind of embarrassing.) Mostly, the firemen played Ping-Pong and cards, watched the *Beverly Hillbillies,* and made lewd comments about Ellie Mae.

Granddaddy was fun at home. As little kids, we'd bug him to death, but he never complained. I loved it most when he'd call the Wizard. He wouldn't do it often, but when he did we'd all gather around. First, Granddaddy would get a deck of cards from the gun rack by the front door (we kept a pellet gun there, just in case). Then he'd say, "Pick a card." We would. Then we'd show it to him. Next, he would dial the phone and say, "May I speak to the Wizard?" After a bit, he'd go, "Okay, hold on," and he would hand the phone to one of us. The voice on the other end would say, "Your card is the six of clubs," and then the line would go dead.

The Wizard was always right. It took me fifteen years to figure out the trick. Turns out . . . well, I promised my granddaddy I'd never tell. A promise is a promise. All I can say is that when I was a kid, the trick would blow my mind.

Childhood is full of mysteries. For me, one of them concerned the house next door, the one I could see from my bedroom window. No one ever lived there for very long. One great thing about transient neighbors is that they don't sink much money into drapes. If they have curtains at all, they're flimsy, thin, and always hanging open. This fortunate circumstance is how my brother and I got to see bras and panties on people other than those in our family.

First, we learned that the people next door couldn't see into our room if we kept the light off. Peering across the side yard night after night we caught many a good bra-and-panty shot. Well, to tell you the truth, we weren't really sure *what* we saw a lot of times, but as long as we spotted white cotton and flesh we counted it. For all we knew we could have been ogling a truck driver parading around in his Fruit of the Looms and a CAT hat. For us, it didn't really matter.

On the other side of our house was a duplex. The McGuires lived closest to us. Mr. and Mrs. McGuire would sit in the living room and look out their window all day long. They knew everything that happened on our street, and even in our house. My uncle Jimmy used to say that he once called up the McGuires and invited them over to dinner, and they said, "Thank you, but we don't like green beans."

Mr. Cunningham lived in the other half of the duplex. He was a grumpy old man who kept any balls we hit over his fence. We'd have asked for them back if we weren't so afraid of him. Cunningham also had a little white poodle named Susie. Nobody liked her either. Susie was one of only two possible old-people-type dogs. The first is the ugly little white poodle with the very pink belly and the lactating eye problem. The other is the Chihuahua with the gray nose and cataracts that is so obese its nipples stick out sideways. Tell me there's *not* an old-people pet store somewhere where you can actually buy only these two animals.

I finally got brave enough to crawl into Mr. Cunningham's yard one night with my trusty penlight. I was eleven and I wanted revenge for all the missing baseballs he'd kept. So I tore thumb-size pieces from all the leaves in his vegetable garden. My plan was to make it look like some rabbit, psychotically depressed at the loss of its tail, had gone on a rampage. Or maybe Susie would be blamed. Unfortunately, old man Cunningham never said anything. If he noticed at all, then, as with our baseballs, he just kept it to himself.

My family has always been funny. My dad has the classic Redneck sense of humor. I remember one weekend when I was ten years old. We were at his farm on the opening day of dove-hunting season. By the time the shoot ended, thirty guys had gathered around the truck, and every one had a beer. (If you can't mix liquor and firearms, what's the sense of being outdoors?) As usual, my dad was up to something. He turned to one of the guys and said, "Hey, let's have a contest. Let's shoot each other's hats."

The guy put down his beer and said, "Aright."

My dad took off his hat and said, "You can shoot mine first." He threw it high into the air. The other guy wheeled his shotgun around and blasted it. The hat jumped a few feet higher, then floated down with fifteen pellet holes.

Then the other guy tossed his hat into the air. But my dad didn't even raise his gun. He just waited until the hat hit the ground. Then he walked over, put the shotgun to the canvas, pulled the trigger, and *obliterated* it.

Everyone broke up laughing. But all I could think of was how my dad was pretty cool and smart and funny. I wished I could also be that way. I guess you have to be careful what you wish for.

My mother's side of the family also had a few tricks to play. When I was seven or eight, Mom's oldest brother, Uncle Jimmy, and I would do improv gigs at the family's covered-dish Christmas parties at the Hapeville Recreation Center. Our act was simple. I'd sit in Jimmy's lap and play the dummy while he played the ventriloquist. Today they'd probably arrest us both for doing that.

Grandma Camp was also a little loopy in a wonderful sort of way. She'd pile up the sofa with pillows, put blankets on top of you, and bring out a TV tray with a huge bowl of sweet coffee— which was just coffee with tons of sugar and milk. We'd take toast cut in strips and dunk it while we watched cartoons. Talk about hyperactive kids.

Grandma Camp also introduced me to TV trays, and I will always love her for that. They were aluminum, with a clay-pot-and-flower design. Soon after we moved into the Hapeville house, my mother decided her parents needed *fiberglass* TV trays decorated with expressions from *Laugh-In*. Things like "Sock It to Me,

Baby'' in weird block letters. My grandparents still have them. There are few things you can count on in life, but those trays are one.

My mother's cousins, Dolores and Buddy, were also two of the funniest human beings alive. Sometimes Dolores would imitate someone she'd seen on TV. Or she would tell wild stories. Dolores always loved the one about the son of the lady who cleaned her house getting arrested again.

Dolores acted the housekeeper's part: She said, ''They framed him. It was not his fault. He had loaned his jacket to a friend. The next day the friend had given him his jacket back, and he was just walking down the street, minding his business. But the police grabbed him and arrested him. The problem was that he had not checked his jacket pockets, and he did not realize that he was carrying somebody else's pistol and $3,000 in cash.''

Or maybe it was only $150 and a penknife. My family remembers stuff and then elaborates. As the years pass we back up each other on our embellishments. It's like the ''guy thing'' that happens when two men are deer hunting. If one year you shoot a spike deer that weighs ninety-eight pounds, then every year the deer gains a couple of points and another twenty-five or thirty pounds. While you tell the story, your buddy, who was there with you, just sits and nods.

''Remember when we shot that twelve-pointer? That deer musta weighed three-hundred-and-sixty . . .''

No matter what, the story will never outweigh the accumulated BS.

This story needs no elaboration. It's one of my earliest comic moments. Perhaps my finest.

When I was ten and my brother, Jay, was five, he had a . . . problem. Not a serious problem. Today he might say it was more of a personal choice. What I mean to say is that he would go days and days without going to the bathroom. My mother worried constantly, when she wasn't annoyed.

We had just moved to Union Avenue when the city decided to expand the airport and build a runway that started at the end of our street. One day after a light rain, Jay and I were playing in the construction site and discovered some particularly nice mud. Not too wet, not too dry, sublimely textured. It was destiny. Rather than wallow in the mud like normal kids, I had a great idea: Build a turd.

We used a two-by-four as our platform. The finished product was close to three feet long. It was probably as big around as two fists put together. This thing would have done Man o' War proud. We picked out all the rocks and tapered one end. We really did a nice job.

After we let it dry in the sun we took it home. I carried one end of the two-by-four and Jay carried the other. We snuck it into the house—maybe the McGuires saw us, but they never said anything—and then into our only bathroom, where we installed it.

We put the blunt end down and stuffed it into the toilet as far as it could go. Then we wrapped it around the bowl once, and brought the tapered end out of the water, almost to the lip of the seat. It looked very much like somebody had forced an anaconda into a fishbowl.

After my brother and I discussed our plan, he nodded and set off to do what I said.

I went into our bedroom, lay on the floor, and laughed for fifteen minutes while he quietly sat in the bathroom, not making a sound. Pretty soon I heard his little voice going, "Mo-om!! Mo-om!!"

By this time I had moved to the closet, where I rocked back and forth with my hand over my mouth. I could hear my mother's footsteps in the hall. I heard the bathroom door open; she took three more steps. I moved from the closet to the bedroom door and cracked it an inch so I could hear. But I could only imagine the innocent look on my brother's face, gazing up at my mother as he slid off the commode. Then I heard her: "My God! Jay, when was the last time you *went?*"

"I think I went last week," he whispered, almost on the verge of tears. He was great. He was perfection. The next thing I heard was my mother rushing out of the bathroom, heading for the hall phone.

"I'm calling Dr. Seevrit. This is not normal."

I staggered into the hall, still laughing, and hit the phone switch hook. Then I told her. "No! Mom! It's not real! We made that out of mud!"

She should have killed us both. But I think she was too relieved to put up much of a fuss.

To this day my brother and I still love to bring up that story, particularly when there's company. "Hey, Mom, remember when we made the fake turd and fooled you?"

She just turns a bright shade of red.

I didn't realize it, of course, but somewhere in my little ten-year-old Redneck brain my future was sealed.

To kids, hygiene is pretty much just a greeting. We brushed our teeth and considered ourselves clean. When I played Little League, I'd rub dirt on my arms and hands between innings. Later when I got out of the tub, the water looked like mud. Dirty water was a badge of honor. The dirtier the better. I'd actually call people in to verify it.

"You think I didn't play hard? Take a look at that tub. Bathed yesterday. Got that dirty today." I had to clean the ring afterward, but it was worth it if I could make a witness say, "Oh my God." I suppose I could have taken a shower, but back then, Rednecks didn't have showers. Well, yes we did, but we called them garden hoses.

When she met my father, my mother was a keypunch operator for the state of Georgia. While repairing a machine in Carole's office, Big Jim, in totally Big Jim fashion, flirted with the girls. He asked Carole out, and three months later they were married. Within two years I was born.

Big Jim has a magic way with women, and he is a legendary figure among my friends. Big Jim could romance women in a convent. You'd drop him off out front, and dollars to doughnuts, an hour later he'd leave with his arm around a nun. Recently, he got married for the sixth time. Each wife has been ten years younger than the one before. My brother, sister, and I are scared that if he gets hitched one more time that we'll be walking his wife to school in the morning.

"Look both ways, Mom."

She'll probably be a good cook, though, with that Easy-Bake oven. I love those cakes the size of quarters.

When Big Jim and Carole were still married, he was a Sunday school teacher and a deacon in the First Baptist Church. When we were old enough to understand, Mom informed us of his other interests. We were living in Greenville, South Carolina, when my mother figured out that Big Jim was fooling around with his secretary. Carole has always seen what she wants to see. Her attitude is "Fool me once, shame on you." By the time she and Big Jim separated, her attitude was "Fool me forty-seven times . . ." Big Jim was just a charmer. If Carole could have put up with Big Jim's ways, I think she might have stayed. In fact, I believe Big Jim could pick up the phone and call any woman he's ever been with, and I guarantee you they would start throwing things in a suitcase and come back.

When the marriage ended, Big Jim moved to Washington, D.C., for a few years, then back to the north side of Atlanta. We moved to Hapeville. Grandma and Granddaddy Camp stayed with us in their house for about six months, and then moved a couple of blocks away. We didn't drive them away. My grandparents just kept moving for the heck of it. They'd buy a house and as soon as they'd get the couch positioned properly in the den, they'd start house-hunting again. They moved six times within a three square mile area before I got out of high school. Apparently, no one had ever explained to them the meaning of equity.

When my grandparents moved out, my uncle Jack, the kindest, nicest human being I've ever known, moved in. A couple of years later my mom remarried. My stepdad's name was Paul. He worked at the same place my mother worked—a distribution center for small, off-brand grocery stores.

We all lived in the Union Avenue house for a while, then moved to College Park. I didn't like living there because none of my friends were around, and soon I started riding the city bus back to Hapeville High. However, I did manage to make a few friends in College Park. One, Buddy Hammond, lived two doors away. To this day, he remains one of my best pals.

With Buddy, you could take the ''might be'' out of ''you might be a Redneck . . .'' Buddy still eats sardines at 5 A.M. with a cup of coffee. He once made his mother a change purse out of deer testicles, as a present. Buddy took the scrotum sack, tanned it, and laced in a drawstring at the top. What mother wouldn't be proud to carry that? (I don't know what he did with the actual balls, but they probably wound up in someone's secret recipe, with butter and salt.)

Today, despite an obsessive interest in taxidermy that sometimes costs him more than his annual income, Buddy is a software specialist with IBM. And he's still a Redneck. Buddy trained himself to wear the wingtips and the jacket and the tie, but he has not been able to give up the chewing tobacco. The boss still yells at him for using a spit cup on his desk in front of other people.

"[spit] You know what you need to do with this here computer? [spit] You need to . . ."

When I was in college, I shared an apartment with Buddy. Our place looked like a salute to stuffed animals. Buddy had actually apprenticed at a taxidermist's one summer and took home everything that nobody came back to claim, including a goat. (Tell me, when is it *goat* season?) But I couldn't blame Buddy for his fascination with dead animals and parts thereof. Taxidermy is a male preoccupation. You never hear a woman say, "You know what would look nice over the sofa? A big dead fish. Wouldn't that look great?"

I've learned that women don't like *anything* from a taxidermist. In fact, if there weren't any women, men would have apartments full of dead, mounted animals. They'd spend the whole day showing them off to each other.

"C'mon in here, George. Take a look at this. That there is a white-tailed deer, a mallard duck, and a Siamese cat. Had to run off the road to hit the cat. They're quick!"

Don't write letters. It's a joke. I have two cats—one on either side of the fireplace.

Pawpaw is Big Jim's mom. She grew up on a farm in Denmark, South Carolina, about an hour south of Columbia. Now she's in her eighties. When I was little, we'd spend about a month with her each summer. The farm was in the middle of nowhere. We learned to milk cows and ride horses, and to otherwise amuse ourselves. (When I got older, amusing myself meant looking for girls. Girls in farm country get bored easily, too.) Pawpaw's brother, Bob, used to say, "When we were kids, we had no toys. We had to learn to walk a barrel." So one summer I mastered walking a trash barrel. Unlike some subjects I had to learn in school, barrel-walking *has* come in handy. You do it all day long in show business.

Another advantage of having relatives who lived on a farm was that we learned to drive early. I started when I was ten years old. By the time I got my learner's permit I'd been driving so many years that it was no big deal. Other kids were proud to do cart-wheels in the living room. I could parallel park before my first kiss. I had the parking down. All I needed was the girl.

Bob taught me to drive. He put phone books under me and I had to stand up on the seat. My first car was a truck with three-on-the-tree, meaning the stick shift was on the steering column. But Bob figured it was no big deal because the tractors had twenty gears. The adults thought nothing of letting kids drive because then you could do stuff for them on the farm. They didn't have time to bullshit around, they needed the help.

It was always, "Take this trash to the dump." Or "Go take the truck down there to Bobby's house, put those shingles on it, and bring them back up here."

My dad taught my brother, Jay, to drive. He took the truck out in the middle of the hayfield and said, "This is how you stop it, this is how you start it. Practice." It was a 200-acre field. You couldn't hit anything. My brother did. He hit a tree.

Jay said, "Daddy, I scratched the truck."

"Right," said Big Jim. "Scratched the rear quarter panel right off of it."

I should tell you right now that I am not the most famous product of my hometown.

Hapeville is where they invented the Chik-Fil-A. It's like a piece of breaded chicken on a buttered bun that, if you put one on top of your head, your tongue would beat your brains out to get to it. It's hard not to touch yourself when you're eating a Chik-Fil-A. We don't have Chik-Fil-A in California, but on the East Coast the mere mention of a Chik-Fil-A guarantees a gasp.

The first Chik-Fil-A was served at a restaurant named the Dwarf House, in Hapeville. I'm not making this up. The outside decor featured the Seven Dwarfs carved out of wood; they were painted and mounted on a movable track. Doug Davis, a Hapeville artist famous enough to have a street—Doug Davis Drive—named after him, had painted the Seven Dwarfs. I'm not sure where Snow White was. But the contraption never seemed to work and a couple of the dwarfs fell over out of sheer boredom. The restaurant also had a little bitty door that we, as kids, were obligated to go in and out of.

Everyone from high school hung out at the Dwarf House parking lot. I had my first sexual experience there, and my first bloody nose. Same night, same person. Also, my first Chik-Fil-A. I wanted no more out of life, except maybe to have a street named after me. And wouldn't you know it, recently Hapeville asked my mother if they could put my name on every city-limits sign.

Like I said at the beginning, I'm a blue-collar guy at heart. Now you know it's true. One reason I make Redneck jokes is, well . . . I have to. Otherwise, having to endure an attitude from the rest of the country that Southerners are stupid and backward would be too depressing.

Apparently we get our reputation because of how we speak. People think they need an interpreter to understand us. I've never met anyone who thinks Southern is the world's most intelligent-sounding accent. When people hear me talk they automatically want to deduct a hundred IQ points. (This may be at the root of many of President Clinton's troubles.) To be honest, I sort of feel the same way. None of us would want to hear our brain surgeon say, ''Aright . . . now what we gon' do is saw the top of yer head off, root aroun' in 'er with a stick and see if we cain't maybe find that dadburned clot.''

You'd say, ''No thanks. I'll just die, okay?''

This is also why Southern financial advisers have such a tough time. Nobody wants to give their money to somebody who talks this way. "[snort] Well, the key is you got to di-ver-si-fy wi' yer money. What we'll do is we'll take half of it, put it in a big mayonnaise jar, bury it out in yer backyard. The other half we'll take down to the dog track and bet on the one that does his business right before the race starts."

I'm still proud of where I come from. We may have words nobody's heard of, but we also have strong values. Most everybody goes to church and is pretty family oriented. Boy scouts, Little League, and scoring points for roadkill are a way of life.

And believe it or not, sometimes we're also guilty of being snobs. We rarely trust someone who isn't like us. We worry about people who would rather go to work than go fishing. But I'll tell you a secret rarely whispered north of the Mason-Dixon line: What we're *really* doing is keeping a good thing going. Our whole image of overalls, no shirt, no shoes, eating grits, chewing tobacco, butt cracks, and acting stupid is intentional and a total farce.

We just do that to keep the rest of the country from coming down here.

What are a Redneck's famous last words?

Simple.

"Y'all watch this!"

Whatever the foolhardy act, his friends always oblige. In fact, they probably put the poor guy up to no good in the first place, just for a laugh. Not that he minds. Men know that their friends are going to get them in trouble. They expect it. That's why they're called friends. Have you ever heard a guy describe friendship? There's *always* trouble involved.

"Ole George, boy, he's a great friend. He'll come get you out of jail at 3:00 in the morning."

That doesn't sound like friendship to me. If George was a great friend his ass would also be in jail, sitting on a cot, smoking a cigarette, going, "She didn't look like no cop, did she?"

The things we do for friends.

I once jumped onto a hay bale, off the back of a pickup truck moving at forty miles an hour. I was seventeen and my best friend, Larry Burns, talked me into doing it. It was easy. All Burns had to say was "You know, there's not *anybody* in the world got the guts to do that." We were at my dad's farm, and already a few underage beers into the twilight. "But I guess if *anybody* had those guts, Foxworthy," he continued, "you'd come closest. But *nobody's* got that many guts."

Five minutes later we were racing through the 200-acre pasture. I tried to keep my balance in the truck bed. We passed the hay bale and I leapt. It *looked* soft—made of hay, right—but it was packed as solid as a rock. I hit the bale, broke my nose, and passed out. I woke up to the sound of Larry laughing. Later, the doctor asked, "How did this happen, son?"

I told the truth. "My friend dared me."

I met Larry Burns in fifth grade, on the first day of school. We instantly became best friends. He can still verify what I was wearing that day: orange plaid pants and an orange shirt with a zipper. I went all out. I figured it would be hard to forget a kid so stylishly dressed. My Southern sense of cool also explained the blue plaid pants and the blue zip-up shirt in my closet—I wore them in the school pictures—and possibly why I was so hot with the fifth grade girls. Because of my fashion sense, Tracey Young and I went together for two or three months. We never touched or, I think, spoke. But that had nothing to do with Tracey and everything to do with where my real affections lay. I was really "going with" Burns and the guys. We were inseparable.

Once Burns convinced me to run through an apartment complex buck naked.

"Jump out of the car," he said, "and Chastain [Danny, the third member of our group, and a year older] and I will pick you up on the other side of the building."

I was such a dumbass. I took off my clothes and got out of the car. No sooner had the door slammed than Burns locked me out, turned on the bright lights, and started honking the horn. I streaked, all right, right into a stand of nearby trees. Then Burns and Chastain drove off and left me. You don't have many options when you're naked in the woods at night. A discarded McDonald's bag starts looking like possible clothing, even a bag for a *small* order of fries.

Was I pissed? Yes, but only for a moment. After all, I could just as easily have put Burns up to bolting through the building wearing nothing but his horn-rim glasses while I pulled the double-cross.

This incident hardly dimmed my enthusiasm for being naked in public. (Only winter weather can do that because what man wants to look like he's carrying around a thirty-cent stack of dimes?) Later that year, Burns, Chastain, and I put on stocking masks and our football helmets and streaked through a high school assembly. We figured we were really clever and mysterious. But two minutes into the next class the PA system crackled to life: "Would Jeff Foxworthy, Larry Burns, and Danny Chastain come to Mr. Givens office IMMEDIATELY!" Okay, so we were caught, but the worst part was that somewhere on the smirk-filled walk to the principal's office we figured out how. Our team numbers were on the backs of our helmets. The saddest thing was that we were some of the smartest kids in the school.

I first heard the term "Redneck" when I played baseball and football for Hapeville High. When we'd compete against teams from Atlanta's north side—the money side—they'd always call us "a bunch of Rednecks." Then, the term was still something of an insult. Now it just means a glorious absence of sophistication. Naturally, we found ways to make the high-society boys pay—with compounded interest.

For instance, every year we'd play Pace Academy, a private school for rich kids, located right by the governor's mansion. Even in the ninth grade, Burns and I were already on the varsity baseball team. We just weren't good enough to start, so we mostly warmed the bench. During the Pace game we watched as their first baseman kept elbowing one of our guys, Danny Beck. Finally, Beck said, "If he does it again, I'm gonna hit the guy." Burns turned to me and said, "If Beck hits the first baseman, I'm gonna beat the crap outta the kid at second base."

Sure enough, an inning or two later, Beck singled. Pace's first baseman used his elbow, and Beck turned around and popped him. The benches emptied and so did the field, as everyone ran toward first base. Except Burns. He made a beeline for the second baseman and blindsided the poor guy.

From then on, and for the next four years, Burns beat this hapless kid, Chad Redman, into dogshit every time we played Pace in sports. During basketball Burns would say, "If I get in, I'm gonna deck Redman." Somebody would shoot the ball, everybody would look for the rebound, and Burns would . . . boom! hit Redman in the stomach. Then we'd have nine guys running down the court and one guy lying in the foul lane.

The weird thing was that Redman always knew it was coming.

We didn't discover why Burns had it in for Redman until our senior year, when someone just happened to ask him. We could never have guessed the reason, but the answer also didn't surprise us. It was pure Burns. "He's got orange hair," he said. "I *hate* orange hair."

Just my luck, I suppose, that he didn't mind orange *clothes*.

Knowing a kid's parents often explains the sometimes irrational acts of the friend you hang out with every day. Even if his ways still make no sense, you at least know what to expect. Later in life, this is why it's a good idea to meet your prospective in-laws long before the word "marriage" is ever mentioned. Just in case there's insanity or a severe case of midlife ugliness in your intended's family, it's not too late to get out and join the witness protection program.

Larry Burns's dad drove a truck that carried cars for the Ford Motor Company. I don't think I ever saw Mr. Burns with a shirt on. He had a gut like the front end of a '55 Buick, only without the headlights. Well, one big light in the middle. His navel was the size of a hubcap. He was a big, big man. Every kid in the neighborhood was scared to death of him, even though Mr. Burns's bark was far worse than his bite.

I remember once I called their house looking for Larry, and his dad answered.

"Hello?"

"Mr. Burns, this is Jeff Foxworthy. Is Larry there?"

"Ah, for cryin' out loud!"

"Something wrong?"

"Eeyeah."

"What?"

"Well, I been watching this movie for the past hour and a half. Guy finally gets the girl. Invites her back to his apartment, they have a few cocktails. They're on the sofa, they start kissing around a little bit. He talks her into the bedroom. Gets her in there, gets her blouse off, pulls her skirt off, gets her naked. He takes his pants off, pulls his shirt off. He's climbing into his bed, he's about to get on top of her . . . and the damn phone rings and it's YOU wantin' to know where LARRY is!''

Another time I went to visit Larry, and Mr. Burns was all smiles and glad to see me. He said, ''Hey Fox! You want some homemade peach ice cream? Just made it.''

''Yessir.'' He handed me this bowl of stuff. I took a spoonful and I can *still* remember that it was some of the worst-tasting glop I'd ever eaten in my life. But Lord knows, I didn't want to offend Mr. Burns. I managed to get the whole thing down and I carried my bowl into the kitchen.

He said, ''Hey, you want some more!''

I said, ''No sir, I'm full.''

''You didn't like it?''

''No, it was really good. I'm just full.''

He started laughing: ''You dumb shit! That wasn't peach ice cream! That's a thing of apricot yogurt. Been in the refrigerator for a couple of months.''

I knew that meant Mr. Burns liked me. Otherwise he wouldn't have wasted his time. He was not a cruel man. In fact, his attitude pretty much explained Larry's way of confronting life. He always had this look in his eyes like he knew something you didn't. It was usually true. I miss him.

I loved hanging out at my friends' houses, especially Deke Cole's. Although Deke's dad had died, his mother was great because she allowed us to drop by at all hours.

At Deke's house we perfected our technique of dropping M-80s down street gutters, just to hear the explosions. Also, because we could hide behind the shrubs near the driveway, we could take a stuffed animal, tie it to some fishing line, and drag it across Jonesboro Road at night, right in front of an oncoming car. You could get some pretty nice-looking skids going. Until you've seen a family of four doing a "three-sixty" in a Ford wagon, you really haven't lived.

By the time we were in the tenth grade, Danny Chastain had become legendary for his gas. On more than one occasion, anyone driving in a car with Chastain as a passenger had to pull over and get out on the roadside, just to prevent asphyxiation. Chastain could clear out an ROTC platoon, even though they knew that if they moved an inch they would have to do fifty push-ups. You *had* to move.

Because of Chastain's prowess Burns and I decided it was only right that we make our friend a World Heavyweight Championship belt in metal shop. We engraved it with those words, and a big cloud. Burns's dad, who made money on the side reupholstering furniture, supplied us with black vinyl. We added metal studs as a final touch.

Chastain was pretty proud of that belt, but one of the cooks at the Dwarf House complained that to give Chastain a trophy without a title bout just wasn't fair. He wanted to challenge Chastain for the crown.

We needed a place to hold the contest. Pete Riggins lived across the street from the Cole's. Pete was Hapeville High's ninety-eight-pound weight class wrestling champ three years in a row. He wasn't big, but he was quick and nimble. Also funny. His dad was the pharmacist at the local drugstore.

We held the fifteen-round championship showdown in Pete's living room. (You learn to entertain yourself a lot in a small town.) Burns and I were Chastain's trainers. The afternoon of the fight we made Danny drink three beers, and his mother, who was also in on it, made hard-boiled eggs and a pot of broccoli. We loaded him up.

Pete Riggins, Steve Raymond, and Doc Riggins were our judges. They even had official clipboards. Now remember, with an event like this we had to *create* the rules because we had no previous competitions to go by. We decided that each guy had two minutes per round to work up his best effort. We judged by sound and stench.

To our complete amazement, Doc Riggins took his responsibilities very seriously. I will never forget him getting up, walking across the room, wafting the odor up with his hand, saying, "Oh my God!" and marking the score on his clipboard. He did this with each attempt. What a great dad. Even if I thought he was totally nuts, I had to respect the man.

I think he was totally nuts.

Burns and I also liked to hold contests at school. One was the King Slob competition. The idea was to determine who could dress the grungiest for a whole week. From Monday through Thursday we were both pretty equally matched: torn shirts, dirty tennis shoes, muddy pants. On Friday I decided to go all out to beat him. I didn't shower, wash my hair, or brush my teeth. I wore my three-day-old football practice undershirt and hunting pants, and added whatever extra dirt I could think of. When I got to school I looked around for Burns, confident I had him beat. Suddenly he walked up wearing the prettiest three-piece suit I'd ever seen.

"You win, Fox," was all he said. That was enough. I heard those words in my head the entire day, while I sat in class looking like the world's biggest dirt pile, and Burns beamed like a million bucks in his new threads.

A major rite of passage in Hapeville was the trip to Shit Creek. Sorry, but that's what we called the two-mile stretch of woods through which ran the drain-off from the sewage treatment plant between Hapeville and Forest Park. The creek wasn't scary in the daylight, but when the sun went down no one was safe.

See, the rumor was that Goat People—half person, half goat— lived in the woods. And Waterhead families: people with *really big* heads. Supposedly entire clans of these freaks existed nowhere else in Georgia but in the woods surrounding Shit Creek. As far as we know today, that's still true.

The older high school kids would take the younger kids to Shit Creek at night. My initiation trip was in Ricky River's Volkswagen. I was in the eighth grade. Pete Riggins, Steve Raymond, and Tom Flood were there as well. We'd driven about a mile into the woods when several guys *thought* they saw a Goat Man on the edge of the woods. Then suddenly Ricky's car broke down in the middle of the road. The timing couldn't have been worse. Goat People and Waterheads were everywhere.

But Ricky said, "Stay calm. It's done this before. All we have to do is push-start it and the engine will kick in."

Warily, we all got out on the dirt road. I swore I could hear the Waterhead families doing whatever Waterhead families did in their houses, back in the dark woods. I stood behind the Volkswagen, ready to push, when suddenly Ricky fired the engine. Flood, Riggins, and Raymond jumped in, Ricky put it in gear and took off, leaving me in the middle of Shit Creek.

I yelled and screamed for what must have been two or three seconds. Then I clammed up. No sense letting the Goat People and Waterheads know *exactly* where I was. Instead, I took off the way we came in. Had someone been standing by with a stopwatch, I would have set a new school speed record.

Everything that could possibly happen to me flashed into my head as I raced through the dark. I knew that calling my parents to come and get me was the least of my concerns. I feared that by the time the Goat People and Waterheads got through with me, there would be nothing left to take home. I imagined the kids at school talking about me the next day:

"Poor Jeff. So young, so funny. So dead."

"And brave. He knew it was coming."

"What do you mean?"

"Don't you know? Before he died he wrote his name and 'I died at Shit Creek' in blood on a big rock."

"The Goat Men and Waterheads have him now."

Of course, my friends were waiting for me in the clearing at the end of the road. I saw the car when I was a good hundred yards away. They sat around drinking Miller beer from pony bottles and laughing like hyenas. When I realized I would make it out alive I did what every victim of this ritual has ever done. I slowed, wiped the snot off my face and the tears from my eyes, and gathered my composure. Then I sauntered up acting all pissed off.

"You bastards! Leave me in Shit Creek! The Goat Man was *right behind me!* He was this close to catching me!"

I don't think they believed me.

Shit Creek was a scary place and it smelled bad. Being left alone there prepared me perfectly for one day getting my own sitcom on television. Stepping out onto the soundstage for the very first time is like being dropped off on that dirt road in the middle of nowhere. Right from the get-go they ask you to push, to help jump-start the show. Then they take off without you. Soon you're crying, you're scared, and you're pretty sure you're surrounded by Waterheads.

"Bomber One to Mother Hen. Come in Mother Hen."

"This is Mother Hen, Bomber One."

"Yeah, Mother Hen. Bomber One requests permission to fire on '77 Ford Galaxy."

"Affirmative, Bomber One. Do you prefer to press or hang?"

"Prefer to hang, Mother Hen."

"Roger, opening hatch. Lock, load, fire when ready."

"Hatch opening . . . Firing . . . Omigod! Direct hit. They're in the ditch! Repeat, they are in the ditch! Granny is out of the car and clutching her heart!''

No, this is not an excerpt from the long-suppressed *Mother Goose Meets Mad Max*. This is the game of ''Search and Destroy'' as played by three crazed teenagers speeding down the interstate in my father's Chrysler (with the electric bomb bay doors—I mean windows), *mooning* innocent motorists. What's even better, it's a true story.

Mooning was a great sport. Nobody ever got hurt. You didn't have to be in shape to play. The fatter you were the more you brought to the window. I'm still not sure why it was such a thrill to make somebody look at our naked butts; I just know we did it compulsively. Unfortunately, any time you mooned someone, you were also open to retaliation. Yes, it's funny to moon, but it's not so funny if it happens when you're with your mother. Once, when I was in the tenth grade, I remember riding to church with my mom, when I looked over to see my best friends drive past with a pressed ham against the passenger's window. Thank God my mom hadn't worn her glasses.

''Oh look,'' she said. ''Uncle Buddy got a haircut. Looks good, don't it?''

We mooned whenever the opportunity occurred. One night, while we hung out in the Dwarf House parking lot, somebody told us they had discovered where Danny Chastain had parked with his girlfriend. They'd spotted his car under a magnolia tree by the mortuary. We immediately gathered ten guys, found the car, took our pants off, and crept closer while Chastain made out in the front seat. Someone counted very quietly to three and BOOM! Every ass was on all available window space. Chastain's date screamed his tongue right out of her mouth. We knew it would take a great deal of sweet talk and Windex to rectify the situation.

Almost nothing was sacred, except that Burns would never moon a car with kids inside. More than once he almost killed himself yanking his ass back through the window because, just as we pulled alongside our intended victims, he'd see a child or even a child's car seat.

"No! No! I can't! There are kids in the car."

If only Chad Redman had been smart enough to wear a diaper whenever he thought Burns might be around.

Church buses were the most tempting targets, but also off-limits. We were God-fearing and figured that if we gave in to temptation that one day we'd have to account for everything. We didn't want the Lord booming, "YOU MOONED THE CHURCH BUS."

"But, sir . . ."

"THOU SHALT NOT MOON. COMMANDMENT FIFTEEN. LOOK IT UP. NOW GET OUT OF HERE."

It was safer to be mooners with morals. But morality had nothing to do with why we didn't moon the girls we knew. Call us practical. Mooning a high school coed wouldn't get *anyone* on the have-to-date chart.

"Oh, everybody's seen his ass. I *must* go out with him!"

Mooning had many derivatives. We called them "BAs" for bare asses, and when we played high school football we cared less about our won-lost record than scoring BAs.

You could do BAs two ways. Drop your pants and bend over and wait for your victim to turn around. Or do the "red eye." A tasteful way of putting this is "a BA with a spreader." Either way, a guy had to admit when he saw it. It was a point of honor. You *had* to concede when you'd been scored upon.

We got bored with that pretty quickly, possibly because we *did it all the time!* So we created more elaborate variations. For instance, every guy knows that there is a complete lack of privacy in most men's restrooms. There are stand-up urinals and sit-down commodes, none of which have doors. This is especially true in athletic locker rooms. Before football practice, two or three guys would always be dropping a couple of "friends" off at the lake, so we'd creep in and do a little number that we liked to call a "train BA." Picture many teenage boys locking arms and bending over, while flashing past an unsuspecting halfback relieving himself in the set position. A common defense against the train BA was to immediately look skyward. That way you only saw one bare ass whiz by, and it didn't count. We defended against that move by silently positioning another man on top of the stall, doing the red eye. The victim looked up and he was had.

The worst BA was the *flying BA,* developed by Harry Hass. His was an ass you just didn't want to look at. Put it this way: Harry was a hairy guy. You've all been to the zoo. You've seen baboons with the same sort of problem. If a nine-year-old had ever seen Hass he'd have thought, "God, if that ever happens to me, somebody please shoot me."

Hass made the most of his gifts. He watched for someone to walk out of the locker room. Then he grabbed the equipment cage wire mesh, swung up, and wrapped his legs around the quarry's neck. We didn't invite Harry to many parties after that.

Did we have too much time on our hands? Yes. In fact, we had so much spare time that we extended the BA wars into the classroom.

Once Burns came into my history class with a note. "They want to see Jeff in the office," he told the teacher. When I walked into the hall two guys were bent over and *I* was history. We finally quit when we realized we had influenced the sub-freshmen. Morals, remember? One afternoon in math class I got bored and stared out the door. There in the hallway was an eighth grader with his pants around his ankles. He was doubled over, and looking between his legs, going, "Fox! Fox!"

I realized I had set a bad example. If he got caught, my conscience would have forced me to visit this kid at the juvenile home. I couldn't do that. They might have invited me to stay.

Another Larry Burns story that cannot go untold.

When Atlanta began building their new airport, Burns got in

trouble for shooting doves under the landing lights at the end of the runway. Apparently the airport authorities frowned upon fire-arms being discharged into the air anywhere near the flight path. Go figure. A sergeant named P. D. Bosket ran him off.

The next weekend Danny Chastain and I listened as Burns told the story. According to Larry, Bosket had said, "If I ever see your ass down here again, even just standing around watching the planes land, I'm going to take you to jail."

Burns was unfazed. "You've never seen this many doves in your life," he explained. "We *have* to go down there and shoot some. The sky is *black* with doves."

For some reason we shared his enthusiasm and agreed to an immediate target practice. At the airport we climbed the fence, shotguns in hand, and sat under the landing lights picking off doves. There were doves everywhere. When we'd drop one, an-other took its place. (Note to the 1996 Olympic Committee. Need doves? Help yourself. They're free and there are still plenty left.)

Suddenly we heard a voice booming through a bullhorn: "Come out with your hands up."

I turned to see two cop cruisers parked alongside our car. We walked out, three geeky sixteen-year-olds, with our hands in the air, holding our shotguns over our heads. We looked like captured soldiers in a *Hee Haw* skit. As we walked, Burns whispered, "Let me do the talking."

No problem. Besides, it's not as if we could have actually hit a plane, I thought. Our guns could only shoot about thirty-five yards and the planes were at least fifty yards above us. That's was at least a fifteen-yard margin of error, which is plenty, right?

The first officer said, "Let us see your hunting licenses." This should immediately tell you something about growing up in Georgia. Then the other added, "What in the world were you kids thinking?"

Burns had already prepared his answer.

"We would have never thought to do this on our own," he said somewhat contritely, "but I have a friend who's a police officer—name of P. D. Bosket—and P.D. said that we oughta come down here and shoot some of these doves at the airport."

The first officer said, "God, I've known P.D. all my life. I can't *imagine* him saying something like that."

Burns said, "Do you think we're *that* stupid to just come down here and shoot doves at the airport? On our own?" Now Larry was indignant. "No! P. D. said it was okay. Think about it. You always hear about doves flying into jet engines and costing the airlines millions of dollars, not to mention endangering passenger safety. I thought—I guess P.D. thought—we were doing a public service."

We had a name. We had the attitude. They let us go.

We didn't always get away with everything.

I'm not especially proud of this story. But I'd rather you hear it from me than read some inaccurate tabloid version that makes me sound like a hick and that will make my mother even madder because *I've never told her any of this before.* (Sorry, Mom.) Anyway, I believe the statute of limitations is up.

Long ago, when I was nineteen, Larry Burns once goaded me in to peeing into the Cincinnati Reds' dugout during a game with the Atlanta Braves. I know what you're wondering: Yes, there *were* players in the dugout at the time. Two, or maybe just one, laughed at the unexpectedly warm drizzle. I feel badly now, but I still like to think that my bravado, stupid as it was, turned out to be a good thing for the team because the Reds awoke that night from a midseason slump and went on to win the Series. They should have sent me a World Series ring.

I learned something, too: Ballpark bouncers *will* ask you to leave. At that point it's actually more of a demand. We were just lucky they didn't take us to jail.

Burns and I should have quit while we were ahead and gone

home to sleep it off. Instead, we hauled down I-85 and I somehow confused the interstate sign with the speed limit sign. When I saw the flashing red lights in the rearview mirror, I said, ''There's a cop trying to get around me. I'm going to pull over one lane, let him around.''

To my big dumbass surprise, he pulled in behind us. As we slowed to a stop, Burns, always the optimist, kept saying, ''Just be cool. Be cool.''

I knew cool didn't matter.

When I was a kid I had once ridden in my dad's car when he'd been drinking beer all day. We got pulled over by the highway patrol. The officer walked up to my dad's window and said, ''Excuse me there, sir. Can I see your license please?''

My dad mumbled something I couldn't quite hear.

''No sir, I don't need a cold beer and I don't think you do either,'' said the officer. ''Mr. Foxworthy, do you know why I pulled you over, sir?

''Nope.''

''Well it concerns that vehicle you're pulling behind you.''

''That's not illegal,'' my Dad said.

''No sir, it's not against the law to tow a boat, but we do require that you put it on a trailer. Now, could you ask your friends to get out of the boat, please, sir?''

My dad protested.

''I don't give a damn if the fish *are* biting. Now, could you ask your friends to get out of the boat?'' said the patrolman.

Okay, that's not a true story. (If you believed it, put this book next to your copy of *The One That Got Away*, by the One-Armed Fisherman.) But it still makes my point.

When the patrolman walked up to me, I tried to be casual. I said, ''Good evening, Officer. What seems to be the problem?'' His answer was to yank the door open and say, ''You going to jail, boys. That's what the problem is.''

Okay, just let me tell my friends to get out of the boat.

He took me around the back of my car, slammed me down, and frisked me. I had a pocket knife about three inches long. He took that away and later charged me with concealing a deadly weapon. You couldn't open a letter with that thing, but apparently the officers felt threatened. Then he took me to the drunk tank at Grady Hospital.

When the drunk tank door locked behind me I suddenly realized that I was scared to death and rooming with people sleeping in their own urine. I thought about Ned Beatty in *Deliverance*. I'm not egotistical about my looks, but I *was* the cutest drunk in the tank that night.

I was also alone. Burns wasn't behind the wheel so he got to call home and go free. I settled down on a bench. Then a guy came over and said, "This your first time in the joint?"

"Yeah." I said it slow, watching for any sudden moves. I thought we were about to dance.

He said, "This is bull. I was in the state pen for twenty years."

"Yeah?" Now I *knew* we were gonna dance.

Then he said, "I'm gonna take care of us."

Time to tango. I started a quick move to the left, but he got up before me, walked to the door, knocked, and told the jailer that he had to use the bathroom. They let him go down the hall. When he returned he said, "Shhh . . . Hold out your hands."

He had collected every cigarette butt out of every ashtray between the drunk tank and the bathroom. Menthol, regular, it didn't matter. I cupped my hands and he emptied the tobacco from each butt. Then he reached into his boot and pulled out rolling papers. He had enough to roll two cigarettes, one for him and one for me. Best cigarette I ever had in my whole life.

Four hours later, the cell door swung open and Larry Burns stumbled inside. It seems he had tried to get me out and he'd raised such a ruckus that they'd detained him for attempting to incite a riot. Before long we were transported, handcuffed, and in the paddy wagon, to a real jail. I was scared but Burns saw an opportunity to have some fun. At the processing center he looked at me and said, "What are you in for?"

I played along. "Going eighty-five in a fifty-five, DUI, attempting to elude arrest, and concealing a deadly weapon. What are you in for?"

He stood right next to a cop. Burns spit on the floor and, as casually as if he'd been arrested for jaywalking, said, "Murder one."

The next morning, Burns' father-in-law-to-be came and bailed us out. It was a proud moment that obviously had zero effect on Burns' engagement, except that his bride's family required him to post bond before the wedding.

Later the police dropped the charges against Burns. I had to get an attorney. I shaved my beard, and we went to court. They offered me a chance to plead *nolo contendere*, but I declined because if you plead it's on your record. Instead, I said "not guilty" and asked for a trial by jury. When the date arrived, no witnesses for the prosecution were present, including the arresting officer. So the judge said, "All right, if you don't get another ticket for nine months, we'll drop every charge against you." That was my plea bargain deal. I signed it, and nine months to the day I drank about 145 beers with Marty Sumpter to celebrate the end of my probation.

I did learn my lesson, though. Afterward I made Marty drive. I know I was a complete idiot for operating a motor vehicle under the influence. I've never done anything like that again, and I'd suggest to anyone out there IF YOU'RE DRINKING, DON'T DRIVE. I got lucky. You might not be.

But that's not the end of the story. I had to go to the weapons bureau and reclaim my pocket knife. They have big wire bins full of bazookas and machetes and submachine guns. I gave a very pretty young woman clerk my claim check and she brought out my knife. She looked at me, then at the knife, and said, "You got to be kidding."

That was the most embarrassing moment of the whole incident.

Larry and Danny were great friends. The only person closer to me is my little brother, Jay. At six feet three and 235 pounds, he is now my larger brother. Jay played linebacker for Duke University, and today he can pick me up with one hand. But he still can't beat me at Sega football. (The preceding sentence will cost me a choke hold.) Can you tell I'm extremely competitive? We often play long distance, over the phone, he at his TV and I at mine. No cheating allowed. And we still have a wonderful relationship. Next to my wife, Jay is probably my best friend.

When we were kids, my mother and sister used to think Jay and I were crazy. (This doesn't seem such a surprise to you *now,* I guess.) One reason was our strong sense of honor. That's not a bad thing. We just had an odd way of demonstrating it. This started very early. We both played sports, and we had a standing agreement that when one guy asked another to smell his socks or his shirt, or whatever, he *had* to do it. If my brother came in from football practice and said to me, "All right, smell this T-shirt," I couldn't fake it. I had to hold up the T-shirt to my nose and inhale. Then I could run around the house going, "Oh God! Oh God, that's horrible!" Then Jay owed me one. The next night I'd go, "Smell these socks."

My mother used to say, "You are outta your minds." I think she knew what she was talking about.

Jay and I constantly invented games. My mother used to say that you could lock the two of us in a room with a thread, a marble, and a pencil, and not only would we come up with a game, we would keep statistics. We played everything: underwear baseball, tube sock basketball. Once, in a highly creative moment in our garage, we decided to throw darts at a whiffle ball bat and see if the darts would stick. I was eleven and my brother was six. I swung the bat as hard as I could at the first dart he threw. The dart hit the bat, turned around, went right back at Jay—and all the way through his ear. Not the lobe, the hard cartilage part. It stuck out the back.

Jay stood there, stunned.

I said, "Does it hurt?"

"No, it dudden hurt."

"What should we do?"

"I think we have to go tell Mom."

I led him upstairs. She was cooking in the kitchen and still had her back to us when I said, "Uh . . . Mom, we made up this game and . . ." I guess she heard something in my voice. She turned around, took one look at the yellow plastic dart in Jay's ear, and said, "I KNEW YOU WERE OUTTA YOUR MINDS!"

She pulled out the dart. There wasn't much blood. I tried to joke about it. I peered at the hole and said, "Look! You can see the dining room!"

"That's not funny," she said.

Oh yes it was.

When I think of everything my friends and I used to pull, I realize that most of it was completely crazy. Yet it bound us together for a lifetime. Boys will be boys, even long after they've become grown men. We were lucky that almost no harm came from our adventures, just lots of good stories. I loved my friends. I remember once looking at the gang and thinking that someday I'd get married, have kids, and a job I busted my ass at and hated, but as long as I got to hang out with my friends (and family) and laugh, that would be my salvation.

Burns and I may have been rascals, but we were also very popular throughout high school, even with the teachers. We may have rushed in where angels feared to tread, but we were always polite little devils when we got there. Somehow we managed to get out of trouble that a lot of other kids didn't even have the guts to get into. I think Burns and I were just full of the youthful arrogance that makes kids believe they can overcome just about any situation. Burns and I were also the funniest guys in school, which made it that much easier to get away with murder.

We were also very strong academically. (Shocking?) He was the valedictorian and I was fourth or fifth in the class. He won the Journal Cup and I won the Outstanding Senior Award. I became president of the student council, and Burns and I were co-captains of the football and baseball teams. My nickname in football was the Flint River Flash. I was very fast, until I hurt my knee. Yeah, yeah, wasn't everybody.

When graduation rolled around, they asked me to make the class speech. I wrote my notes on index cards, then I practiced and practiced. I got so I could flip the cards in order and recite the speech without looking. I just had them for reference.

During the ceremony, I asked Burns to hold my cards for a minute while I went up to receive some award. That was a mistake. During the speech I began to lose my place. I knew I was on the fourth card, so I looked at my notes to see what came next. But instead of seeing card number four, I saw card twenty-three. I flipped it over and the next one was card number two. Then eighteen. Burns had shuffled the deck and he made me look like a total idiot. All I could hear while I fumbled and stammered was someone behind me laughing and, finally, falling off his chair.

I didn't have to wonder who it was. I knew in my heart that as I'd stepped to the podium, Burns had probably whispered to everyone within earshot, ''Y'all watch this.''

I would have done the same thing.

After all, what are friends for?

Say It with Krylon

What's the sexiest four-word sentence in the English language. I'll give you a clue. It's when a Southern woman says, ''Hey, y'all, I'm drunk.'' Any woman from anywhere *could* say it, of course, but it's highly unlikely that she also fantasizes about some guy in a baseball cap laying on top of her, cooing, ''Who's yer daddy, sweetie? A'right, sweet thang.''

Southern women *are* different.

Where else can you find a woman who can chug a Miller pony

beer, chuck the bottle out the window, and hit a road sign— without having to sit up?

Where else, when a woman gets mad, is the full impact of her fiery temper expressed as "I am so mad at yew"? True, it doesn't have the same impact as a housewife from New Jersey screaming, "Get your ass in the car!" but it means far more. The image of Southern women may be all fluttery and delicate, but it's just that steel magnolias get pissed with style. Instead of telling you to get into the car, she'll wait until your back is turned and drive the car into *you*. The really tough ones do it when you're looking.

By far the biggest difference between Southern women and all others is their Southern daddies. These men know why you're at their house. You can't bullshit them a bit, which might seem strange since these are the same men who will swear they were once abducted by aliens and forced to undergo a thorough body-cavity probe. (And wished they could have taken a probe home as a souvenir to use on the cat, or the wife, or on the next hunting trip.) But when it comes to their daughters, you can pet the dog, know every football stat for three decades, and actually *be* from another planet, and good old dad will still be ticked at you for sniffing around his baby girl. He knows you're there for the same reason he was somewhere himself, twenty-five years ago. He knows your mission is to get his daughter into the same state in which she came into the world . . . naked.

(Word of warning: I'm now a Southern dad and you better not be coming round my house in about fifteen years.)

It's easy to fool Southern moms, though. (We fooled them when they were daughters and nothing's changed, right?) Sweet talk about how wonderful the mashed potatoes, gravy, and rabbit stew taste works every time. Unfortunately, unlike Eddie Haskell on *Leave It to Beaver,* Southern men have to prove they mean what they say by actually eating the stuff.

However, here's the good news. Whatever you must endure to date a Southern woman, she will compensate you for your hardship and make it worthwhile. Southern women are truly the hottest creatures on earth, even with the windows open in midwinter. Their butts don't get cold until *after* marriage. Here's the good deal: You don't have to woo them much. Southern romance does *not* necessarily mean you have to buy presents or take your date somewhere nice. Saying, ''You're prettier than a blue tick hound,'' will do just fine. Or, for that special occasion, ''Your feet don't stink near as badly as my brother's.'' When you fall in love with a Northern girl, you have to send her flowers and candy and cards. When you fall in love with a Southern woman you just spray-paint her name on a water tower, an overpass, or a big rock—it all depends on your town's tradition. But this much is universal: Whether it's having sex or catching a fish, it doesn't mean anything until you tell someone. True love means "Say It with Krylon.''

I once was so in love that I spray-painted a girl's name on the outside wall of the high school gymnasium. Unfortunately, it was only four feet off the ground. Not too impressive. Eye level does not equal everlasting passion. To have real impact you must stand a damn good chance of dying in the trying, or at least of walking with a limp for the rest of your life. In Hapeville the water tower was the true-love proving ground. If someone climbed to the top in the dead of night—during daylight the cops got upset—to declare his ardor, everyone knew it was serious.

By the way, the key word in the preceding sentence is ''everyone.'' Less than an hour after the sun rose on a new name on the water tower, *everyone* in town knew the young folks involved. Once, after a midnight spray-painting run, I walked down the street and a complete stranger said, ''Hey, nice job on the water tower last night.''

I grinned and never heard the words ''water tower'' at all.

I liked girls early. Just about every young lady in the fifth and sixth grades wore my ID bracelet. Well, every cute one. It meant we were going together. It didn't mean we ever spoke on the phone or appeared in public together. Maybe we'd indulge in some intense cross-classroom staring during homeroom, but that was about as steamy as it got.

My only problem was that I was too shy to approach a potential steady myself. So I'd get Larry Burns to do it for me. Larry, as you know, would do anything.

I'd say, "Larry, will you ask Ellen Harrison if she'll go with me?" A while later he'd come back and say, "Yes, she'll go with you."

"Okay, give her my ID bracelet."

Two weeks later Larry would hand back the bracelet and say, "Now she's gonna go with [insert boy's name here]."

Thank goodness Larry took his job seriously or I'd have had to spend *all* my allowance on cheap jewelry.

This is the only advice that my father, Big Jim, ever gave me.

"Son, the day will come when women won't sleep with you on a $1,000 bet. I don't care if it costs you your job or your health or your life: When you get on a hot streak, ride . . . it . . . out."

It was a *Father Knows Best* moment. I swear.

Otherwise, Big Jim didn't tell me much about women or, on a more basic level, sex. We never had the conversation parents should have with their children even if the children know more than their folks. Of course, I would never know as much as Big Jim. His mother once swore to me that when he was six years old, she'd caught him in a cornfield doing "something" with a local girl. Can you imagine that? When I was playing with GI Joes, Big Jim was playing with . . . no. It's not a picture I want to think about. No wonder he never told me about sex. He probably just assumed everyone did it at six.

My mother never told me about sex, either. I guess she was easily embarrassed. It makes sense. She went to church five days a week and is still the most conservative woman I know. Instead of a frank discussion about procreation (a strange word since we all begin as amateurs), my mom decided to bring home a pamphlet for me from the pediatrician. It was about boys turning into wolves. I didn't get it. I checked the mirror for facial hair. Seeing none, I decided not to worry about it.

Fortunately for everyone, I learned about sex on my own, and in the same way most boys do: in the street. Late one afternoon, during the summer before the fourth grade, my next-door neighbor, Brad, sat next to me on a curb and discussed the facts of life. Brad and I were the same age, but he'd already gotten the facts. We *knew* they were the facts because they came straight from his older brother, Rick. Rick was in the *sixth* grade. Then Brad said that Rick had a telescope. Now I knew for sure that he knew.

According to Rick, sex went like this: You got married. Then you got in your car, drove to a place where there weren't a lot of other cars, and parked. Then you unzipped your pants, you got on top of your wife, you put yourself inside her (he didn't elaborate about exactly where), you peed, and you drove back home.

I was perfectly fine with all of this.

My only question was why it had to be in a car. Why couldn't you do it in a house? But Brad said that's the way it had come down from his brother, and we knew that it had to be right.

Later that night I lay in bed and thought about the glories of sex. I also knew I'd forever miss them because there was no way I could ever pee inside anybody.

I knew you put ''it'' in ''something,'' but I didn't know exactly where or what that something was. I finally learned when one guy in our group—yes, it *was* Larry Burns—reported on an actual close encounter with that particular animal.

He stunned us with its location.

Larry said, "It's much lower than you think it is."

We had previously imagined that the girl's "it" was almost like a second navel, but Larry set us straight. Then we couldn't get it out of our minds. (I've also never gotten over how he'd actually encountered the real thing in the eighth grade.)

Until then I'd been satisfied just watching cheerleaders jump high at football games and wishing that I owned a bike so I could date. Now it was even worse. I had to have that bike!

As a kid, I often wondered how you could ever sleep with somebody and then, without giggling, actually speak to them *in front of other people*. Wouldn't you only think about what you had just done, whether it was five minutes or five days earlier?

Boy, life teaches you how wrong you can be. It's *entirely* possible. Not only can you do it with somebody and look at them without giggling, you can also change your phone number and move just to get away from them when they start making plans for the rest of your lives together.

"I'm sorry. The number you dialed is no longer a working number. Please check the number and try again. This is a recording."

I kissed my first girl in the first quarter of the ninth grade. I also shot my first squirrel then. Cross your fingers that I don't get these stories confused.

Carrie Ann Campbell (the girl) was a real cutie at College Park High School. She lived three blocks from me, and one day I asked if I could walk her home. She said yes. Standing on her front steps, I kissed her—*smack*—quickly. She didn't seem to mind, so I did it three days in a row. On the fourth day, before I could kiss her, she invited me in. I'd have felt like Casanova had I'd known who Casanova was. Instead I felt like Barney Fife getting lucky. Inside,

I was about to kiss Carrie Ann in the hallway when she stopped me and said, "Wait. You don't know how to kiss."

Suddenly I felt like Barney Fife in a swirl of skunk vapor at point-blank range. Then Carrie Ann surprised me and said she'd show me how to do it right.

I am *so* grateful.

French kissing was amazing. Back then I could kiss Carrie Ann for four hours and do nothing else. Or possibly I was just rationalizing because I figured that there was no chance in all of Greater Atlanta that Carrie Ann would ever let me do much of *anything* else. No, I really didn't mind. I've always been a pragmatic guy, interested in investing for the long term. If I could kiss Carrie Ann for four hours, perhaps one day she'd let me rub the outside of her sweater. So what if my faith in the future was remarkably similar to that of a contestant on *Let's Make a Deal*?

"Do you want to risk everything for what's behind door number three, or do you want to keep what you've got?"

I wanted to keep what I had. I didn't want to go too far and have a girl say, "You know what? You're an animal. You're not getting *any* of this. I'm taking away the kissing *and* the outside of the sweater because you tried to go *inside* the sweater."

Now, of course, everything has changed. I read in the newspaper that the rule at some colleges today is that people who want to make out must ask permission to move ahead *each step* of the way. I don't think this would work in the South.

HE: *Can I kiss yer neck?*

SHE: *Oh, baby.*

HE: *I'm gonna stick my tongue in yer mouth.*

SHE: *Only a little . . . Oh God . . .*

HE: *Where does this damn bra unsnap?*

SHE: *Here, let me.*

And later . . .

HE: *Why the hell cain't you wear jeans with buttons?*

SHE: *It's not my fault that the zipper's stuck. Now get off me you . . . you . . . fat . . .*

HE: *But baby, you know I luv yew.*

SHE: *Hold on. What's that smell? Did you spill Buck Lure in this car?*

HE: *Worked, didn't it?*

Let me catch my breath.

Carrie Ann and I were as seriously involved as ninth graders could be, but being from Georgia I know that there are also kids who, at that age, are actually having baby showers. Pregnancy and parents with shotguns can really make the ninth grade hard. I was lucky with Carrie Ann because her parents never interfered. To be honest, I never actually *knew* how her parents felt about me because I'd never met them. I've since realized that Carrie Ann had no parents and lived in her big house all alone.

My routine with Carrie Ann Campbell was pretty much: get up, go to school, get out of school, kiss—we'd sit on the couch for hours after class, just making out—go home, eat dinner, go to bed. Sometimes I'd call her at night. We even exchanged ninth grade photos. I didn't write "I love you" or anything on the back. I just signed my name.

One day, after a couple hours of swapping spit in her basement, I finally put my hand under Carrie Ann's sweater. I'm lying. *She* put my hand under her sweater. It's the truth and an important lesson: Long term investment pays off. Guess what? She was wearing another sweater. But hey, if door number three opens, you stroll on in. At that moment life really, really changed. I walked home from her house and passed a woman watering her lawn. I looked at her and thought, "You know, I *know* what I'm doing now. You'd better be careful. I could wreck your home."

Carrie Ann and I went together until I decided I missed the guys at Hapeville High and started riding the city bus back there. Long distance relationships don't work, and Hapeville and College Park were four miles apart. Four miles is too far to ride a bicycle, especially when you can't spend the night. So we had to break up. It was tragic and it took Carrie Ann at least a couple of hours to get over me.

Carrie Ann ended up with Buddy Hammond. There was even talk of getting married someday. His wedding gift to her was going to be a set of handmade, all-leather luggage with fur handles. Buddy's grandfather died still wondering what had become of his prize milk cows and his squirrel tail collection.

Even if I hadn't switched schools, my romance with Carrie Ann would have ended. I was ready to say, "I think we should see other people." You realize, of course, that nobody ever says that without actually *having* another person in mind.

I had my eye on Kellie Joyce, who lived in Hapeville. She was a year older than I was. Kellie and I had talked while sitting on the grass outside the public tennis courts, and I had a pretty good feeling that she would kiss me had I not been involved with Carrie Ann. So "I think we should see other people" meant for me to go home that night and call Kellie Joyce.

Kellie agreed to go out with me. I went to her house and met her parents. She actually *had* parents, which was a new thing for me. After I'd settled into their living room couch, her dad said, "Now, who is your mother?"

Having a conversation with a dad is uncomfortable. (A dad hanging around is unusual. Usually, the Southern father unloads a couple of mean, knowing glares and then sulks quietly away to the garage.)

"Carole Foxworthy."

"What was her name before she was married?"

"Camp."

Her dad jumped up and said, "Your mother is *who?*"

I repeated myself. "Carole Camp."

"What's her phone number?!" he said. I gave him the number and he started dialing. I thought, "Oh my God, what have I done?! Mom's got a prison record I don't know about!" Turns out both Mr. and Mrs. Joyce had gone to high school with my mom.

"God, isn't that ironic," Mrs. Joyce said. "Twenty years later and now our kids are going out."

I later found out that Kellie was my half-sister, which made her even more appealing.

I'm kidding.

If any of you still wonder whether I'm a true Redneck, this long-repressed secret should convince you. Believe me, I never thought it could happen to me. A long time ago, *I was attracted to my cousin.*

We were only fourteen and we had spent the day at a family reunion. You know the routine: swim and hang out all day, and then eat lunch off concrete picnic tables. Afterward, she and I took a walk and pretty soon we were kissing. I don't know how it happened, but I do know my brain was screaming in my ear, "You idiot. You're kissing your cousin!"

Of course another part of me was also screaming: "*Second cousin.* C'mon, she's almost a stranger! Haven't seen her in six years!"

We cooled down short of sin and went back to our families. We didn't talk about what happened and have never discussed it since.

I later found out she was *also* my half-sister. Apparently Big Jim had had the same problem a generation earlier.

Again, just kidding.

When I was in the eleventh grade I finally went out with Betty Calloway. Every guy talked about Betty Calloway. She was stunningly beautiful. Lucky for me she was also Chastain's cousin. I have never been more nervous with a woman than before that date. I might as well have been dating Elle MacPherson *and* Cindy Crawford and their twin sisters.

We went to see the movie *Where the Red Fern Grows*. Short synopsis: dirt poor Appalachian family. The kid wants coon-hunting dogs. They have no money. The kid cuts fields for a penny. Takes him five years to save enough money. One night he runs away, takes a train, goes to this town, and buys two bloodhounds: Old Dan and Little Anne. Carves their names on a tree. Comes back and raises these dogs. They end up winning the state coon-hunting championship.

One night not long after that, they're hunting and a cougar attacks Old Dan. They take him back home, try to nurse him. He dies. They bury Old Dan in the yard. Then Little Anne will not eat. She just lies out on Old Dan's grave and moans. Pretty soon Little Anne dies from a broken heart. They bury her next to Old Dan.

Soon the family decides to move on. They're loading up the wagon and the boy says, "Let me go say good-bye to my dogs one last time. At the beginning of the movie, the kid's mother had told him a story: "And the place where the greatest love on earth is," she said, "a red fern will grow." So he runs over the hill and there, between the two mounds of dirt, grows a red fern.

Now, I am dating the most beautiful girl in Hapeville High and I am sobbing uncontrollably. This movie made *Ol Yeller* look like a comedy. I cannot quit crying on our first date. This is the saddest story I have ever seen. We're driving home and I'm *still* crying. I'm so broken up I didn't even care about what Betty thought of my blubbering.

Finally, I parked in front of Betty's house and started kissing her. By the way, parking in front of your date's house is, contrary

to conventional wisdom, a very smart move. You can get away
with almost anything. Even if her parents look out the window and
see someone's heels pressed against the left rear passenger window, they don't *really* see them because they can't imagine you'd
have the nerve to try and climb on top of their daughter *right* in
their own driveway.

As for Betty, she kissed me enthusiastically. Apparently, not
being ashamed to let her see me get in touch with my female side
made her happy to let me get in touch with her female side. In
fact, the kissing was so hot and heavy that she got light-headed
and had to take a moment and stand outside to catch her breath.
That was it for the kissing. In fact, we never went out again.
Turned out she had the flu and I'd turned the car heater up too
high, but it was a running joke that I kissed her so well that she
almost fainted.

Technique is everything.

First you kiss for three hours. Then you move your arm up on
her arm. The goal is to have the inside of your arm accidentally
brush the outside of her breast. If she doesn't shift away, you may
move on. "Okay, wait a couple of minutes and bring the arm back
. . . Oops, bumped it again. Still okay. Okay, now let's see if we
can put our hand on her side, between her waist and her chest. Still
doing okay . . ."

The whole procedure is like monitoring a space launch.

"Okay, let's gently ease the hand up. T-minus-8, 7, 6, 5, 4,
move, grab." Many times that's when a young woman will launch
a preprogramed counterattack and stop your hand, or move it back
to its original position. With any luck her primary systems will
fail and her secondary systems will be forced to take over, and
your hand will be cleared for takeoff.

Often, I would proceed to T-minus-four seconds and reverse
course and start again, with ever so slight variations. It was confus-

ing and satisfying. The idea was to wear a girl down. Eventually, they got damn tired of stopping you.

Too bad it never dawned on us that perhaps our objects of desire might have *wanted* what we wanted as well.

As I matured sexually and socially and began dating regularly, I made some important discoveries. For example, girls in the country were easier targets than girls in the city. Girls in the city had other stuff to do. They could go to a movie, they could go to the mall. Girls in the country didn't have a whole lot to look forward to. So whenever I went on vacation or down to the farm, I immediately began looking for prospects.

I figured that out the summer between the ninth and tenth grades, when I went to Pawpaw's farm in South Carolina. I met a girl who was the friend of a friend and we were all going to ride horses. She was cute, with blunt-cut blond hair. After a morning on horseback, she and I tied our mounts outside my uncle's trailer. No one was home. We went inside to get something to drink, settled down into the sofa, and she shifted right toward me.

I liked to think I was just too charming. On the other hand maybe she figured that making out with me was better than cleaning up after the horses, or the usual country pastime of staring all afternoon at a tree. Like I said, there wasn't much to do. Anyway, she pretty quickly let me put my hand inside her shirt. Not only did I feel it, I saw it. It was so cute. You know how you open up a blanket and you see a puppy for the first time? So innocent, and it's looking right up at you. That's all we did, but it was enough.

Later Uncle Bob and I milked the cows and talked. Uncle Bob said, "Hey, you guys were gone for quite a while," he said, with a devious chuckle. My mind churned. Suddenly I had my first shot at actually getting a man's approval.

"Oh, yeah. Yeah." Remember, this is my *uncle Bob*. And we're *milking* a cow.

"So, how was it?"

"Good. Good," I lied. "Really good."

"Did you . . . ?"

"Oh, sure. Sure."

"You dawg."

His reaction taught me an important lesson: Lying works. I'm just glad Bob wasn't so impressed that he wanted to demonstrate any advanced techniques on the cow.

We always hear how men like to swap tales of a graphic sexual nature in the locker room. This is completely true. However, we can be more subtle. Occasionally we simply like to brag about our hot moves.

Whining is always at the top of the list.

HE: *Please, sugar dumpling, please.*

SHE: *No. Uh-uh. No way.*

HE: *But my girlfriend just don't understand me like you do.*

SHE: *Then break up with her.*

HE: *Cain't. She's also my maw.*

SHE: *You're sick!*

HE: *Me? Sick? You did it with your cousin!*

SHE: *I know. But he's nice.*

HE: *But sweetie . . .*

Even though this example is assumed to be true only in select regions of the country, guys everywhere are *still* pathetic. They prove it every year at spring break. My most vivid memory is of five guys crammed into a Camaro, going to Fort Lauderdale or Daytona Beach, saying, "We're gonna get some. We're gonna get some." Then six days later, "Next year. *Next year* we're gonna get some."

Nobody ever got lucky. It took me two or three spring breaks to finally figure out what I'd been doing wrong. Like everyone else, I'd been too overeager. Hollering things at women didn't work. And for most women projectile vomiting has never been a turn-on. Finally, I tried a different tactic. When we all went into some place selling quarter drinks, I let the guys roam the bar while I sat by myself at a table and acted uninterested. Within five minutes I had eight coeds saying, "Why are you just sitting here? What's wrong with you?"

Anything that works.

Travis Tritt's road manager showed me the all-time best way to pick up a woman. We did a show at the Omni for the Super Bowl when it was last in Atlanta. I noticed that he had on two different cowboy boots: one was red lizard, the other tan buckskin. I said, "Why do you have on two different boots?"

He said, "I've gotten more women doing this than I can handle. All I have to do is go out dressed like this to a bar. I don't have to say a word. Women just come up to me and go, 'Why do you have on two different boots?' *They* start the conversation."

Like I said, anything that works.

Men are hounds. We think nothing of dating someone who just broke up with our best friend. I once asked a friend if I could date his ex. He said, "Don't you recall me telling you about her chasing me through the parking lot with a butcher knife?"

"Yeah," I said, "but she's *really* good-looking."

DeWayne Twilley, another good friend of mine, once brought a girl to my house for me to meet. He said he just wanted to show her off because she was so damn pretty. He was right. But a sophisticate like Twilley should have known better. (In the land of guys with no shame, Twilley was the king.) The minute he went to pee I wrote down my phone number and told her to call me later. It was just one of those things. I knew she liked me and I liked her as soon as she walked in the door. After Twilley took her home, she called me and we talked from 1:00 in the morning until 5:15 in the morning. Then I went to meet her. I didn't even care that she lived across the street from Twilley. (Sorry, DeWayne.)

Some of the best advice I got about dating and women came

from a little guy named Morris, who worked in the Kroger deli. "There's nothing free," he'd always tell me. "Nothing free, buddy. Always got to pay the price. Nothing free."

I always tried to remember Morris' advice at the end of dates where I knew I wouldn't be calling again. I had to because otherwise I'd give in to the devil himself and think that although I had no intention of asking the girl out a second time, well, hell, I'm here and I got nothing else to do, so I'll make my play. Maybe I could get something for free. I had to force myself to remember that if I was successful, there'd be a price to pay. It might be tearful telephone calls or the girl showing up at work unexpectedly. Carrying my baby. With her dad. Who had a shotgun. I had to learn to let it go.

Although my testosterone level overflowed, I never wanted to be like all the other guys, who I figured were pawing their dates and not taking no for an answer. That it worked for them didn't seem to matter to me. I somehow believed that after the heavy breathing was over and the girls were back in their frilly bedrooms clutching a battered Barbie and scribbling the evening's events in their diaries, that they somehow resented these overly-aggressive boys who had once again overwhelmed them with whining persistence and taken advantage of their virtue.

Boy, was I full of it.

In fact, my desire to be sensitive just made me lose girls to the bad boys. I don't know why I persisted in believing that by being the nice guy I'd win. I guess I thought that finally one day a grateful woman would lie on my bed and say, "You know, you're such a nice guy, I should just take off my clothes and let you lay on top of me." Unfortunately, no woman ever had that realization.

DeWayne Twilley had been there, and done *that*—the whole thing!—by the ninth grade. His first woman was a junior at Hapeville High. They did it on her couch. We were pretty awestruck, and we all wanted to date her, but she wouldn't give us the time of day.

DeWayne was our idol. DeWayne was always bold. Once, in college, we were out at a club. I sat at the bar making nice small talk and trying to score with a pretty young woman. DeWayne said almost nothing. Suddenly he spoke up, but not to me. "You know what? I really don't want to kill the whole evening. Would you like to screw?" She said, "Yeah," and they got up and left. De-Wayne got his face slapped a few times, but more often he left with a woman on his arm, and he didn't come back.

I don't know how DeWayne did it. No, that's not true, I know how he did it, I just never understood what the women saw in him that made them go along. I mean no insult to DeWayne. He was one of my best friends. He wasn't bad looking, but he was also nothing to write home about. I guess he just had the Big Jim touch, which very few guys are blessed with. It's almost a curse, because then you have to end up telling stories while the rest of your buddies go, "And then what'd she do?" DeWayne was in the middle of our circle for many years, and the rest of us were on the outside going, "And then what'd she do? Oh my God. Wait, back up, back up."

Eventually I caught up. Patty West was the girl of my dreams. She'd dated a "bad boy" and it didn't work out. So our Spanish teacher set us up. I can still remember what Patty wore on our first date: a pair of double-knit peach-colored pants, and a brown sweater with some tan deer on the front. She had just gotten her hair cut that day in a little blunt swoop. She looked like a million bucks and she smelled great.

We went to see *Rocky* at the Varsity, the world's largest drive-in. We parked on the upper deck. Pretty soon we started kissing, and we were really, *really* kissing. I had misjudged how much Patty had wanted to kiss me, and thought, "This is easy city here.'' So I put my left hand on her right breast and she instantly got upset. She yanked my hand away and said, ''You're an animal. I thought you weren't that kind of guy, and here you are, first date, and you're groping me.''

I said, ''No, I'm not that kind of guy! You know I'm not that kind of guy. I don't know what happened.''

Maybe the heater was on too high again.

She forgave me. Patty and I continued to date, and I swear I would not have touched her breast had you balanced a million dollars on it and said ''Take the money.'' I might just brush up against it accidentally, though.

We went out, on and off, for three years. Eventually, I got to touch her *there*. The Friday before homecoming we parked off the driveway to the community swimming pool in Hapeville. She took my hand and put it on her breast. (Why fix a method that's not broken?) It was nice.

That Saturday we made out on my dad's couch. I got bold and started to unbutton her pants. To my surprise, she lifted her rear end off the couch to help me slide off her jeans.

She had on another pair of jeans underneath.

Or she might as well have, because instead of focusing on what was about to happen, Larry Burns's voice popped into my mind, explaining his theory that the moment a guy always remembers is not when he has sex with someone for the first time, but ''when a woman lifts her rear end to help you take off her pants.'' When Patty West raised her hips I knew I was going to do it. My brain overloaded. ''I'm going to do it. I'm going to do it.'' Then a couple of seconds later, ''Oh damn, I just did it.''

Afterwards I knew it wouldn't count if I didn't tell someone. Naturally, I called Burns, even though it was three o'clock in the morning.

''Guess what? You're not going to believe what went on tonight.''

''No, you didn't.''

"Damn right I did."

"How long did you last?"

"Almost six seconds."

I was like an antiaircraft flare. They don't burn long, but boy, they are brighter than hell and it takes no time at all to reload.

Patty West was also the first girl to whom I'd ever said "I love you" and meant it. I may have said it to Carrie Ann Campbell, but that's just because she let me put my hand between her sweaters. Otherwise, I've always tried to avoid trading terms of endearment for sexual favors. I never wanted to be known as a guy who would say *anything* just to get what he wanted. I wanted to get it without having to say anything at all. So I took that bullet out of the love gun, and that weapon out of the arsenal. I've always played fair. I have never been a game-law violator.

I like to hunt within the rules.

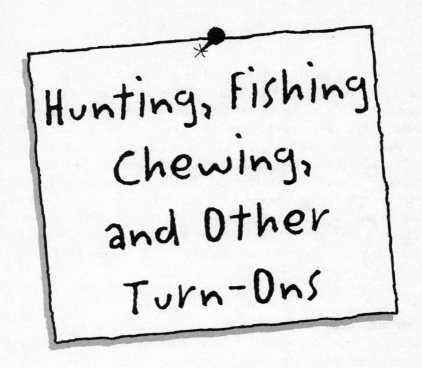

Hunting, Fishing, Chewing, and Other Turn-Ons

All men delight in pursuits that disgust women. Hunting is near the top of the list.

No woman, not even my mother nor my wife, can understand the pleasures of rising before daylight, in subfreezing temperatures, to sit in a tree for four hours, waiting for the chance to shoot an unsuspecting deer. I can spend an entire vacation doing that. I have.

Hunting makes a man more male. If he kills a deer, a man will cover himself with as much blood as possible while gutting it. Then he'll bring home the carcass and let it sit out in the open. Men know that blood and carcasses drive women crazy. After a week, a dead squirrel or possum on the coffee table is guaranteed to cause marital problems. A dead deer can be grounds for divorce.

Men who don't hunt can also upset that special someone and be included in this virile brotherhood. Simply slice your finger on a beer can pop-top, and smear the blood everywhere. Then use the half-empty can for an ashtray, and let the carcass stand out overnight to allow the three odors to mix and create a sweet perfume that will render an entire room uninhabitable to women for at least forty-eight hours.

Men hunt deer from deer stands. For the uninitiated, "stand" means a platform in a tree, maybe fifteen feet above ground. You drive spikes into the tree trunk, climb up to your private perch, and then wait for a deer to wander by. The stand is a sacred place, the sportsman's holy ground. No blasphemy intended, but I still have one question: How come it's called a stand when all we do is sit?

A really good stand depends on its location. A really *great* stand has its own mailing address. Being close to those places deer frequent helps immensely. Also important is the platform's condition. Wood rotted so badly that every time you sit on it you take your life into your hands rates high. It means the stand is productive.

Since we hunters spend so much time in trees, it's fortunate that the stand is also a good place to think. Thinking for me usually means writing jokes. Another favorite place to write jokes is on a long car trip. It drives my wife crazy because I have to write longhand, which is pretty tough when you're going seventy miles an hour and you've got a notebook on the steering wheel. I'm careful about doing this now because my wife will inevitably scream,

"Just let me out of the car!" So I wait until we're driving at night and she's asleep.

There are very good reasons to be in the tree. First, you don't have to employ camouflage, as you do when you're waiting in a duck blind. Second, sitting up high reduces your chance of getting shot by other hunters who've mistaken your Day-Glo orange parka and red hat for a deer. Third, deer don't often look up. Even deer can't understand why somebody would spend his vacation sitting in a tree.

At its most basic, waiting in the deer stand is a rite of passage to manhood, very much like chewing tobacco and sex, though not as messy. We'd sit in our stands from about half an hour before daylight until ten or eleven in the morning. Then we'd climb down, go back to the house, and eat breakfast. We'd lollygag around the den for a bit, swap sightings and "almost" stories, and then head out for a couple of more hours. The rule was that you had to sit in the tree until it got too dark to see your hand in front of your face. This, in turn, led to another adventure: shooting at noises.

I first hunted with my dad. We'd set out in the pitch-black dark woods and I'd never admit to him how scared I was. At first we shared a deer stand. However, the only father-to-son knowledge that passed between us in those memorable and sentimental moments was when I'd say, "Dad, Dad . . . ," and he'd whisper hard, "Be quiet." You had to learn to settle in and be still.

One day my dad let me sit in a stand on my own. He picked one near his and I felt safe just because he was close. As I got older, he'd park the truck and go, "All right, you go into the stand over there at the bottom of the creek, and I'm going to be over there on the one by the cornfield." Then I'd have to take the flashlight and walk by myself through the woods. I'd always do something like step into the middle of a covey of quail, which would then explode. Only my laundry man knew for sure how scared I really was.

When men hunt together, the first thing they do is jockey for stand position. My dad had about thirty stands on his property. Some were in good shape. Some were comfortable but in a bad location. Some had no redeeming qualities except that they were actually up in a tree. Who got which stand was a seniority thing. It started with my dad and his guests and worked its way down to the youngsters. Usually, I sat around drinking coffee in the dark, cursing while guys picked among the better stands.

"Tom, where do you want to go?"

"Ah, I think I'm gonna go down there to that stand right there behind the pond."

ME: "Damn."

"Bub, where do you wanna go?"

"I'm gonna go down there to the other end of the hayfield and take that stand right there on the fence."

ME: "Jeez."

Then, after everybody had chosen, my dad would turn to me and say, "Okay, you got the one in the backyard by the basketball goal."

"But Dad, I'm not gonna kill a deer by the basketball goal! Deer don't even like basketball."

Even so, I've never wasted my time hunting. You see the woods wake up. You hear a noise, it stops and it starts. Maybe it's a bobcat, or a hawk or a fox squirrel. An hour and a half later you suddenly see something flick, and you realize it's a deer's tail at the top of the hill. And then it's gone.

Today some of my happiest memories are of hunting and fishing with my dad. I know now that I was a pain in the ass to take, and that I cut down his chances of being successful. Yet he cared enough to take me with him. Whenever I did something good, he was the first one I wanted to show. I'd always think, "I want to go find my dad."

Some time during this age-old ritual, if you get very lucky, you see a deer. Actually *shooting* one is like winning the lottery. I didn't get my first deer until I was a college freshman.

It happened on opening day of hunting season. I was in my stand, an hour or so after daylight, mulling over the big questions of life—like bacon and eggs, or more beer for breakfast. I looked down absentmindedly and saw a deer six feet away. I'd never even heard him coming. And he wasn't moving.

So I blasted him.

Larry Burns heard the shotgun report, came running over, and we stood around and admired the dead animal for half an hour. Then we got the truck, drove it into the woods to get the deer, and got the truck stuck in the mud. We had to trudge back to the house and ask my dad to bring *another* truck and a shovel to get ourselves unstuck.

Our troubles didn't dull our enthusiasm for the kill. Deer hunting is cathartic. I know guys who have hunted a hundred times between deer kills, and yet they keep coming back. Here's one secret reason why: The biggest thrill of deer hunting is *not* actually killing anything. No one *really* expects that. What the guys want to know is what you *saw*. After four hours up a tree, breakfast is just a bunch of guys stuffing their faces and saying, "Bill, did you see anything?"

"Nah, I didn't see anything."

"Tom, did you see anything?"

"Yeah, I saw two does about 9:00 A.M."

You had to list what it was and the time, what it did, and how long it stayed around. That was enough to get you back out the next weekend. If somebody saw a buck, that was enough to keep you coming back all year.

Our hunting reports were very much like sex stories. Once you get it, it doesn't really count until you tell everybody every detail.

That's how you learned that there were different degrees of serious hunters.

For instance, Big George was one of the unluckiest hunters among my dad's friends. George was five foot six, weighed 310 pounds. Good shape for deer hunting, right? George loaded trucks down at the Pepsi plant. He was bald and very funny, and the first guy I ever knew who had a monster truck. He let us drive it and that made George a really good egg. But through the years it became clear that George was the only guy in camp who had never killed a deer. However, there were some "almosts."

"I saw a buck."

"Where were you, George?"

"Well, I was down there behind Skeet's house, down in that cornfield down there."

"What happened?"

"Well, I'd been sittin' there for about forty minutes, and I looked up, and saw a big buck jump the fence. He looked like a six-pointer, maybe seven even. He just stood there, eating right at the edge of the soybeans. So I picked up my gun, turned down the radio, lowered the window . . ."

"Wait a minute . . . you're *in the truck?*"

"Yeah, and I'd just turned the heat back on."

No wonder he'd never killed a deer: George drank coffee, smoked, and listened to country music with the truck running. None of those ingredients are listed on a bottle of Buck Lure. I know because I've bought all that stuff: Buck Lure, Doe In Heat Lure. You're supposed to put it on your clothes with the hope of attracting a deer. I think one was nothing but deer urine.

That's another female turn-on.

"Oh, if you could just wipe some of that doe urine on you, *that* would really get me hot."

After you kill a deer, then what? Clean it. Eat it. If the buck is particularly impressive, visit the taxidermist. Gazing at the face of your adversary forever frozen, right above the fireplace or the marital bed (in the kitchen or guest powder room is bad taste), warms the hunter's heart. I've mounted and displayed my share of trophies, but my *favorite* deer-head story is about the one I gave away.

After college I worked at IBM. I first worked in dispatch, answering the phones and handing out service assignments. One of the guys, Ray Stubblefield, hailed from Florence, Alabama. Ray was a big deer hunter and I learned a lot about the sport from him. Every time he came to Atlanta, he would bring a stack of pictures of himself with these incredible trophy deer. We all believed that Stubblefield was the greatest deer hunter in history.

We were all wrong.

What we didn't know then was that while Stubblefield rode around all day as an IBM serviceman, he also kept a camera in his car. Any time he saw hunters with a nice kill in their truck at a gas station, at a country store, or at a meatpacking plant, Ray stopped and asked if they would take *his* picture with *their* deer. What kept us off the scent of this bighearted imposter was that he made sure he never wore his regulation IBM uniform—suit, white shirt, tie, wingtips—in any picture. Apparently he kept a camouflage jumpsuit in the car. I've always meant to check, but I believe all Florence, Alabama, males of hunting age had to keep at least one camouflage jumpsuit with them always. It was the law.

Ray's desire to impress didn't end with his IBM colleagues. He'd pose with these celebrity deer and then send the photos to regional magazines like *Georgia Outdoors* or *Alabama Outdoors,* for their camera corner. Soon Ray was a hero to hunters throughout the Southeast. Ray's freezer was empty, but he owed the film processing people his annual salary.

When Ray came to Atlanta for a few weeks that coincided with deer season, I invited him to come down to my dad's farm one weekend. I got lucky and shot a deer. It was a little spike. The horns were more like two half-pencils. In the middle of cleaning the deer and wondering what it would taste like, Ray asked me what I was going to do with the head.

I said, "I'm gonna throw it away." It certainly wasn't one I would mount.

Ray said, "May I have it?"

"What do you want it for?" I asked.

Ray had an idea, which he shared with me. It was so wonderful that I *had* to give him the head. Then he took it home and froze it.

Turns out Ray worked with another guy named Garrett—Garrett Quartier. Quartier was a very serious guy and much more strait-laced than Stubblefield or me. After Stubblefield went back to Alabama, Quartier came to Atlanta for two weeks for an IBM class. He asked Stubblefield to look after his house and feed his cat. On Stubblefield's last night he took the deer head out of his freezer and put it in Garrett's master bathroom toilet, and shut the lid.

Try to picture what happened. Garrett Quartier came home, settled in, and eventually went to the bathroom. As he took a seat, he happened to glance down and there, between his legs, is a deer head looking up at him. Garrett Quartier swore that he had never been that scared in his entire life.

That's also when they discovered that Garrett Quartier had a heart murmur. His doctor prescribed medication and he avoided any further serious complications. It was Stubblefield's idea, but my deer head, so I'm taking half-credit for saving Garrett Quartier's life.

It's five o'clock in the morning and he's waking me up. But it's hard. It's summertime, I'm ten years old, and this is supposed to be vacation. The days of rest and relaxation. Then my eyes squint open. I can barely see his face, lined and ancient. But I'm happy. Very happy. Today my granddaddy and I are going fishing.

He creeps into the kitchen while I put on the clothes I selected the night before. Blue jeans, but not the good ones; instead the jeans I hoped would later that day bear the mud stains and the fish smell. It almost seemed like a rule. The more disgusting the clothes the better the day had been. If Mom made me undress on the porch before I even dared enter her clean house, I knew it had been a wonderful day indeed.

The shirt couldn't be white. Granddaddy said it spooked the fish, so I'm wearing my old blue football jersey. It is full of holes and has been placed on the forbidden schoolwear list. A dumb call in my opinion because this is one cool shirt. The numbers on it are white, but I'm banking on the fact that fish can't read.

I find my way into the kitchen. He has made me a cup of coffee. Lots of sugar and lots of cream. I can't imagine anyone drinking the stuff any other way. I bet none of my friends are drinking coffee this morning. I bet they won't drink coffee for another eight or ten years. I watch as he finishes loading up the cooler. There are no wasted movements. This is a task he has perfected over the years. You do something a million times, you learn to get it right.

The menu rarely changes. A thermos of ice water. Four Coca-Cola's in the little bottles. A few packs of peanut butter crackers and two ham sandwiches. White bread. Mustard and mayonnaise.

He tells me to get my coat. It's always cold before the sun comes up. Even in July. I grab my zip-up sweatshirt with the hood. I wish I had a jacket like his: a blue jean jacket with a red and black flannel lining. The jacket bears many miles, and they're not highway miles. I've never seen another one quite like it. He and the jacket seem to belong together. They fit each other.

Granddaddy unlocks the camper top and slides the cooler into the back along with the rest of the gear we loaded the night before. Everything has it's place. The cooler goes in back of his tackle box, but in front of the trolling motor battery. I always insist on carrying the battery to prove I am a worthy fishing companion. Man, is it heavy! But I will never say so out loud even though I'm sure my labored stagger must give it away. I don't think I've ever picked up that battery without a warning not to spill acid on myself. Through all the years I've never seen one drop of anything come out of that battery, but I fear it nonetheless. Granddaddy's warning always makes it sound like the acid will burn a hole clear through my leg before I can even get my pants off. Very scary stuff.

He is a very methodical driver. I not sure of very many things in life, but I would be willing to bet everything I own, Ted Williams model baseball glove included, that he has never gotten a speeding ticket. Sometimes I have to glance down to make sure he's actually mashing the gas. I assume that he is because the black work shoe is resting on the pedal. Black work shoes with white socks. If he has another combination I've never seen it. Granddaddy is a man of few fashion surprises. I find the consistency to be comforting.

Our trips are never cluttered with chitchat. When he talks it is to brag about having the fastest radio in Georgia. He turns it on and off twice to back up his words. I'm confident that they don't hold contests to determine such things, but I still can't imagine anyone capable of proving him wrong. This is one fast radio. And it is always set to the same station. WSB AM, "The Voice of the South, with all the latest in news, weather, and sports." He always seems to be most concerned about the weather. I guess it's true what they say, people can always find something to worry about. I don't really care if it rains, I just want to catch a fish.

I can't remember riding with Granddaddy where he did not find at least one opportunity to pull the same corny joke on me. He points down the road and says, "There's your name on a sign. 'Old Stopper Head.'" Of course the sign really reads "Stop Ahead," but it never fails to make the two of us laugh. It's just one more reason I know the old man likes me.

We have a few regular fishing holes. Most of them are small ponds located on the property of different farmers he has met over the years. He always stops at the house to confirm that it is okay that we fish. I am required to go with him and to say "Thank you *for letting us fish.'' We are always extra careful to lock gates and to never leave a mess.*

Being the passenger, the opening and closing of the gates usually falls on me. I always hope that cows are not lingering too close to the gate. It's not that I'm afraid of cows, it's just that I don't like them to get too close. I've never heard of someone being killed by a cow, but they are big, and they have a funny way of looking at you—always with one eye. Cows never look you directly in the face. It's like they have a plan of escape, and they are just trying to work up the nerve to pull it off.

When we reach our fishing spot we unload the gear in the same fashion we loaded it: meticulously and painstakingly slow. But I'm always in a hurry. I worry that the fish will stop biting at any moment. Time is of the essence.

We always put the tackle boxes and the rods and reels into the boat last. Granddaddy's tackle box is roughly the size of a small barn. I'm sure it carries one of everything ever designed to entice a fish. Sometimes when the fish aren't biting I entertain myself just looking through it. I'm always asking what different things are, and he usually explains, and follows with a grand story of a fish that fell victim to it's charm.

My tackle box, on the other hand, is about the size of a shoe box. I have painted my name and a picture of a bass jumping out of the water on top of it. It contains mostly the cherished discards from his box. There are a few lures I have bought myself—all replicas of the ones he holds in highest regard. Unfortunately, they never seem to catch nearly as many fish as his lures do.

My rod and reel is also a hand-me-down. It's old but in fine working order. His are the paintbrushes of a master. A Shakespeare Wonder Rod supporting an open-faced Mitchell reel. He has three of them. All exactly alike. I'm sure that if the manufacturers knew, they'd be flattered that he has picked them as his tools of choice.

I am always amazed at the ease and accuracy with which he

casts. *Granddaddy will always say something like, "Well if I hadn't of throwed right there I never would have caught this one." Then with the flick of his wrist he sends his lure sailing through the air and it comes to rest inches from a semisubmerged log that should have a sign painted on it that reads "Home of a monster bass." I try to emulate his technique, but I spend lots of my fishing time trying to pull my lure out of the limb in which it is firmly anchored. "Trolling for tree bass again?" I hear him say. This always fills me with a slight degree of panic. I don't want him to have to stop fishing to help me. Not that he ever seems to mind, but I am afraid that he'll one day grow weary of his fishing partner's ineptitude and chose someone with the ability to keep his lure in the water instead.*

He always catches more fish than I do. Usually about fifteen to my one. How can he be so lucky every single time? When he hooks one he really seems to enjoy reeling it in. As he cranks he gives a play-by-play commentary complete with estimates about the fish's size, where he hit it, and guesses about what the scoundrel might do to avoid eventually joining us in the boat.

On the other hand, when I get lucky enough to hook one, I retrieve it with all the calmness of Barney Fife making an arrest. There is no savoring the moment. I reel so fast and pull so hard that I have been known to make a fish go airborne. You should see the look on a fish's face when he breaks the water, sails over the boat, and resubmerges on the other side. "He looks like a pretty good one" I hear my granddaddy chuckle. I ignore him, because this is no time for jokes. If I don't get this thing into the boat then I have no proof that I actually caught one. After all, who's going to believe a fisherman? It is understood, too, that if I actually do get him in the boat he is going home with us. Catch and release has no place in my ten-year-old vocabulary.

If I am fortunate enough to add one to the stringer, I must then continually check him out.

"Put those fish back in the water," I hear him say.

"I'm just looking at them" I reply. Even on a stringer with twenty or more fish I am always able to pick out mine. I know exactly what he looks like. He's usually the cutest one.

It is then as I'm staring at him that I am always filled with a little pity for the fish. Not because he started the day in a cool lake playing fish games with his friends and will end it wearing a cornmeal jacket in the bottom of a frying pan. I feel pity because he fell to me instead of the old man. What a stupid fish he must be. Imagine the shame his family must feel as they tell the story to their friends and loved ones. "It wasn't even the old man! It was the goofy kid in the football jersey!" Their friends gasp that fish gasp and say, "Oh . . . We're so sorry."

The fishing day always ends following a long period of no action. It has to be that way. Never has a fisherman left the water while the fish are biting. It's physically impossible because that is what fishing is really all about. This hope goes out with each cast: Maybe this will be the one that hooks the fish of a lifetime.

We conclude much the way we started, only in reverse order. We are careful to leave the place as we found it. Granddaddy says "That's how you get to come back." We pick up trash and lock gates. The cows aren't anywhere to be seen. God is looking out for me. We always stop back by the house and thank the folks for letting us fish on their place. Granddaddy always offers them our fish, while I silently pray that if they do take some, mine won't be in that number. Thankfully, that has never happened.

We return home to the ceremonial showing-off of the catch. Granddaddy is much more low key and humble in his approach than I am in mine. By that I mean that he doesn't leap from the truck, grab the stringer, and go running through the house screaming, "Look what I caught! Look what I caught!" Of course he is also spared the lecture from my mom about how hard it is to get the smell of dripping fish out of the living room rug.

Finally, I am required to help Granddaddy clean the fish, though it is a job I don't mind. The combination of scales and entrails are enough to make the football jersey truly disgusting. I wear the mess like a medal. It is a proud moment.

Job complete, we head back into the house. Already I am growing excited and planning our next trip, the trip that may net one of us that fish of a lifetime. Granddaddy knows what I'm thinking. He musses my hair and smiles. I hope I can go fishing with him forever.

Years later, standing in the river, watching my line bob up and down in the current, I often thought about those trips with Granddaddy. Compared to my fishing expeditions with Burns and Chastain, they were an island of tranquillity.

Fishing with the guys was about as tranquil as the day Atlantis sank under the ocean.

Once, the three of us spent the day catching nothing. Finally, Chastain got a live one and reeled him in. But instead of letting him go or putting him on the stringer, we just left the fish hooked to the line and put him back in the water. Then we fished for another fifteen or twenty minutes. Still, no one got a bite. But we had planned ahead. We took the rod with the fish out of the water and passed it to the next guy. Then he slung the fish—still on the line but rested now—back into the river about fifty yards so *he* could have the thrill of catching something. After an hour of this, the fish wised up and as soon as he hit the water he started swimming for the boat as hard as he could. Eventually he just skied in on his side, not even fighting anymore.

Another time, we caught a bunch of fish and brought them back to the house in a bucket. I'm not sure why, but for some reason we forgot about them. We should have cleaned the fish because real sportsmen never keep anything they're not going to eat. But something more important came up—probably a car wreck we had to see, or maybe somebody's field was on fire—and we forgot our catch.

The next day we discovered our bucket of *really* dead fish. That was the first and only time we played fishball. One guy batted, another pitched, the third narrated.

"Here's the windup, the stretch and . . . *fish on the way*. Ohhh! He was looking for a catfish, threw him a bream."

When the batter connected it was really disgusting. There's nothing like the way a fish disintegrates when it meets a Louisville Slugger going the other way.

"Oh! He got all of that fish!"

The pitcher got covered with scales from head to foot. I think that's why fishball never really caught on. Plus, it's hard to turn a double play when the fin is between first and second, and the head's just tripled down the right field line. However, you do get a truer fish bounce on AstroTurf than on grass.

We made important discoveries while fishing. For instance, you can pee off the side of a boat and still catch a fish. Whereas, if you pee out of your deer stand, your day is pretty much over. Also, with fishing you pretty much eliminate the possibility of dying every time out. You're not going to get shot. No hunter will mistake you for game. Even if you're a kid wearing a moose costume to school on Halloween, it's a good bet that carrying your lunch box where it can easily be seen will keep even the most aggressive sportsmen—like those waiting for a deer to wander near the elementary school—from firing spontaneously. But if it's safety you're after, I'd stick to fishing, where the worst injury is a fishhook in the ear.

Trout fishing involved a practice called "looping." It's not about tying lures but about getting the best position in the river. The idea is to always be upstream of everyone else. So if you saw one of your buddies going around you, you'd cut up through the woods and go around him. Not only did you then get first crack at the fish but you also totally screwed up the catch for anyone downstream. The problem is that fishing spaces you out. So it's pretty disheartening to see a guy upstream, loop him, and discover that you've been looped by *everybody*.

Should nature call when you're out in the wild, you have to use whatever accommodations are handy. Especially at night. On one fishing trip we all had a big argument with Buddy Hammond about how far away from the tent we should be to use the "restroom." It was a matter of honor. You were supposed to take your toilet paper and go out in the woods somewhere. We knew that if you could still touch a tent flap, you weren't far enough away. But not Buddy.

"Oh, for God's sake, Buddy! We gotta sleep here, you dumbass."

Other than that, Buddy was the Marlon Perkins of outdoor hygiene. I've always admired Buddy for that, and for sharing his wisdom. If you forgot your toilet tissue, he knew which leaves made the best substitutes, which had a nice texture, and which wouldn't just crinkle and disintegrate. He also knew which leaves were poisonous. The stories of how he acquired that knowledge would make your skin crawl.

Burns never listened to Buddy, or learned from him. Before I left the house, the last thing I always did was grab a roll of paper and stick it in my coverall pocket. Burns, for some reason, never grasped this concept. When we were deer hunting, we could put Burns on his stand before dawn and come back four hours later and he'd be wearing a shirt with only one sleeve.

We knew the answer even before we asked the question.

"Oh, man, I had to go bad."

"But that shirt cost twenty bucks! Toilet paper is eight cents, you idiot."

You know the cut-off sleeve look that Bruce Springsteen made popular? I wouldn't be surprised if he'd found a shirt Burns had worn hunting twice, at a garage sale.

My father always used to fish with my grandfather, and both of them used to fish with me. Now that I'm a father I sometimes fish with my two young daughters. Just carrying on the tradition, I guess. Last month I learned you can get goldfish out of an aquarium using a Dustbuster. That's the most efficient fish-catching device I've ever seen. Next time we go to the lake, I'm taking a Sears ShopVac. Not only will we catch our limit, but we'll leave the outdoors just a little cleaner than we found it.

Hunting and fishing are fine, but to really be a man you had to chew tobacco. I first tried it in the ninth grade. Everybody else on the baseball team did it so I figured I might as well. I adapted pretty well, although it's never been the most charming taste in the world.

For those of you not familiar with the wonderful world of chewing, here's a few facts you ought to know:

1. Chewing tobacco is not pipe tobacco. It's more like wet, sticky leaves. Okay, mulch.

2. A real chewer will open his pouch with a screwdriver, stick his face in it, and just pull out the tobacco with his teeth. Most of us aren't that sophisticated, or willing to answer impertinent questions if someone sees us trying this in public.

3. Most people can only chew on one side of their mouth or the other. It's a lot like masturbation: There's not a lot of swapping off. You pick your side and you stick with it.

4. To get a chew going you pull out a handful and pretty much eat it. You put it all into your mouth and you work it around with your tongue and your teeth, until you get it into a little ball. Then you take the ball and stick it outside your teeth, but you leave a wedge of tobacco that goes between your teeth. You chew and suck on that, and spit out the juice until it gets down to nothing.

5. Chewing doesn't get you high, but if you get a good chew working, you may suddenly start hearing Hank Williams songs go through your head. Don't panic. Sing along.

Dip is a little different. It's fine-grained, more like cigarette tobacco. Walt Garrison said it so well: "A little pinch between your cheek and your gum." But when it comes to the quality of spit, dip spit's not very good. It almost looks like spit, whereas *chew* spit can ruin somebody's brand new boots. We learned that pretty quick. Just for fun we'd wait until we saw somebody with new hunting boots or tennis shoes. Then we'd walk by, never say a word, and PFFT! land a gob on their leather uppers. Took the new right out of their footwear.

"You bastard! I paid eighty bucks for these!"

Chew spit will also take out the hurt and the poison of a beesting. And it's great for making an exclamation point at the end of a sentence.

"So what'd you do after you spit on his boots, Jeff?"

"I told him to kiss my butt." PFFT! "But only if he could catch me." PFFT!

There's a fine art to spitting, and we were its masters. If a guy wasn't listening while we talked to him, we could easily spit on his shirt without him even knowing it. You just had to make the spit as silent as possible. To do that, put your fingers up to your lips, like you're holding an invisible cigarette, spread them a bit, and PFFT. Spit on a guy's shirt is not a pretty sight, particularly in church.

When we played baseball we would take Bubble Yum chewing gum and loosely wrap a string around the chew to hold it. But you had to be careful if you ever slid into a base. You *did not* want to swallow the chew. You'd spend the rest of the day vomiting. Even swallowing only a little juice can make you turn green, and your buddies red with laughter.

My favorite use for chew was to make Larry Burns sick. Knowing the secret ways to gross out your friends to the point of hurling was powerful knowledge when growing up. Forcing a friend to dry heave could make you happy for a long time. Larry was immune to so many things, but once, when Burns, Chastain, and I were building a fence down at my dad's farm, Chastain and I discovered Larry's weak spot.

We took a break and I said, "Burns, would it make you sick if Chastain and I exchanged chews?"

"Don't do that!" he said. Right then I knew I had him. I immediately pulled out my chew. Chastain did the same. We traded and stuck them in our mouths. Larry ran off and dry heaved into the creek bed. Chastain and I gave each other high five after high five. By the way, Burns deserved it. Just to make someone sick he'd do things like walk through the cow pasture and pick up a big handful of cowshit and go, "Anybody wanna eat this?" and stick it right up to your face. You'd go, "Oh my God!" and try to control the vomit impulse.

Years later I learned that Burns's real kryptonite was snot. The best I ever got to him was one morning while deer hunting. We were walking through the pitch-black woods, and all I could think about was how Burns had lately done horrible things to me. I had a bad cold, and so I did one of the grossest things I'd ever done. We've all done it as little boys: Hold one side of your nose and blow out the other.

I followed Burns through the woods, slowly blowing my nose into my mustache. Snot and a mustache are a lethal combination. When we got to his deer stand Burns said, "Will you hold my gun while I climb the tree?" and I said, "Fine." It was dark. We couldn't see each other. Then I said, "But before you climb the tree, do me one favor and look at this." I turned my flashlight on my face. He fell to his knees at the bottom of his own deer stand, dry heaving. I didn't care if I saw a deer that morning. I had dropped him.

As with hunting, chewing tobacco has never been a big hit with women. The gals we dated knew we chewed, but we also knew better than to load up around them. I've never heard a woman say, "You know what I really like about Jeff? It's when he *chews that tobacco* and it makes his breath stinky and his teeth yellow. And we have little cups full of spit all over the house. That's such an endearing quality."

Instead, we'd hear, "I'm not kissing you, you've been chewing."

"How can you tell?"

"Well, you've got spit all over your shirt."

"That's not my spit. Burns got me."

"Oh, in that case, kiss me, you fool."

We never tried to get the girls to chew, either, unless for some reason we also wanted to make them puke. Besides, any woman who could get the hang of chewing wasn't on our "must date" list. In fact, any woman who chewed tobacco (a) didn't prefer men or (b) men didn't prefer her. Any day now, just to make my life miserable, I'll expect a picture of a gorgeous woman I could never get to first base with chewing tobacco.

Of course, these are just fond memories. It's been a while since I've chewed. It's not easy to do with a wife, kids, and job.

"You might be a Redneck if . . . PFFT! . . ."

Not much of a career in that.

Masculine habits and the sporting life all prepare a young man for joining the adult world and for that most human of pursuits, the biological mating imperative. When we succeed with the opposite sex we like to think it's something we've done on purpose, a move we've practiced, or an element of our personal style that turned the trick. But as any hunter knows, achievement is really more a matter of patience, persistence, and luck. The last, more than anything else, was the rationale behind Big Jim's reminder to always ride out a streak no matter what the cost. I've always considered that sage advice from a versatile hunter.

I once had a lucky streak that's never been repeated. Even if I tried to mess things up, I couldn't.

I'd spent a week hunting and was driving back to Atlanta from the farm, down I-20, in a beat-up green pickup truck. I had a mounted deer head in the front seat beside me. I hadn't showered for four days, so it was probably hard to tell me from my passenger.

Suddenly three young women in a car pulled alongside and motioned for me to roll down the window. Of course, I did. For a moment no one said anything. I looked horrible, they were laughing, and I figured it was at me because I was the only one in my car with a stupid smile. Then the prettiest girl said, "What kind of guy would ride around the interstate with a deer in the car?"

I said, "What kind of girl would *talk* to a guy who's riding down the interstate with a deer in the car?"

She laughed. I said, "You should call me later, we'll talk about it." Remember, we were hollering and going seventy miles an hour. I said, "Here's my phone number." I didn't even ask for hers. When I got home, she called. She said, "Come over. I want to talk about the deer."

I said, "Let me take a shower. Where do you live?" An hour later I was at her place. I had one drink. She said, "Excuse me a minute," disappeared into her bedroom, and came out in a bathrobe.

As I sat there in shock, I thought of all those times I'd prayed for the biggest deer to walk within range, or for my cast to hook the fish of a lifetime. This wasn't quite that, but it was close enough. I looked up at the apartment's cottage cheese acoustic ceiling, imagined I could see through it to the blue sky above, and thought, "God, I didn't even *try* for this. Thanks."

Clearly, men also delight in pursuits that please a woman.

With any luck it's sometimes even her idea.

It's Nice Work, If You Can Avoid It

Finally, the day your folks warned, promised, and usually threatened would come has arrived. For better or for worse your whole life changes.

I'm not talking about holy matrimony. This is worse.

No more allowance.

Out of gas and oil for the old Plymouth Duster? Need cash for dates? Want shells for the .22 and tobacco to chew? Bowling ball need repair? Forced to pay your own bail on a drunk and disorderly warrant?

What's a twenty-one-year-old to do?

Time to get a job. Time to see if Vern down at the garage thinks your talent for hot-wiring luxury vehicles can be bent to fixing them as well. There's lots of good jobs available. Besides, things could be worse. Just remember that somewhere, someone else is doing something with hot tar for five dollars an hour.

Thanks to Big Jim, I have a strong work ethic. I've always wanted to pay my own way and support my family. I like the freedom money in my pocket affords. Yet the conventional wisdom is that when the subject is work, Rednecks want to change the subject. People think we're lazy. The truth is that we're salt-of-the-earth working men and working women, even if the salt gets a little soggy in the humidity.

Then to what may we assign the blame for our slothful reputation? Once again: our accents. It's understandable. When it takes someone three times as long to make an excuse about why he's late for work—for the fifteenth time—it just *sounds* shiftless. But is that really fair? I don't think so.

It's hard work to come up with a believable lie.

By the way, I'll be a bit late coming in for this chapter. I slept in, but if anyone asks, I'm saying my pet goat got ahold of my alarm clock and ate it. I don't want to waste your time, so while you're waiting for me to shower, dress, have coffee and breakfast, read the paper, run a few errands, and maybe catch a matinee, I'll be happy to pass along some wisdom I've gathered about the art of lying to get out of work. I know I'm getting ahead of myself. I should probably talk about *working* before I get to the *lying*, but a good lie is like a good joke, and I can't resist a good joke. Both require forethought, timing, and a surprise ending.

Let's say you hit the snooze button fourteen times and you're running fifteen minutes late for the job. First, if you actually *show up* only fifteen minutes late, you're going to look like you kept hitting the snooze button. So relax. Sit, read the paper, drink a couple of cups of coffee.

I'm sorry. I can't go anywhere without my day-of-the-week undershorts, and I can't find Monday. (Musta been a great weekend.)

Now, for the lie. Don't use the standard, "I got stuck in traffic." They'll know you're lying. Think of something that is so bizarre that your boss will honestly feel sorry for you.

I don't recommend the dead relative lie for two reasons. First, it's hard to keep up with whom you've killed off and who's still living. Grandma can only pass away so often, although in some families like mine—remember, between Big Jim and Carole, they've been married nine times—there can be plenty of Grandmas to go around. But then up crops the second problem: guilt. If you're like me, saying, "Uncle Fred got hit by a train," will make you worry that Uncle Fred *will* get plowed by a locomotive. Then you'll be up on a murder rap for knowing way too much. So if you use a relative, don't kill them. A serious illness is just fine, and it could keep you out of prison.

I'll be out of the bathroom in a minute. I've still got to brush my tooth.

You can always claim that you're sick, but be sure to name an illness about which no one would dare ask questions. Projectile vomiting is acceptable, but explosive diarrhea is my personal favorite. That should end all discussion on the matter. If pushed, mumble something about "bad sausage," then say, "Oh-oh, here it comes aga . . .''

If you decide to feign personal injury, I recommend wearing an Ace bandage. Stuff an old T-shirt under it to simulate swelling, and moan constantly for effect. Make sure it's a believable injury. Falling in a corn reaper is too much if you only plan on being out for a day or two. Plus, strapping your arm to your side so your empty shirt sleeve can flap in the breeze will eventually become a big pain in the ass, possibly tear a rotator cuff, and ruin your fly-fishing cast.

I swear, I think the dog ran off again with my car keys.

What you really need is a story that will not only excuse tardiness but encourage your boss to give you the *entire* day off. With pay. How about this: "The sewer backed up into my house, the furniture is floating, and I can't find the kids." Who would expect you to work while your couch is drifting away. It's just bizarre enough to possibly be true. That's all you're shooting for anyway: possibility. Once you create a reasonable doubt for yourself, you are home free. So to speak.

Should anyone give you the third degree on your return to work, don't hesitate to become indignant and stomp out of the room. Crying is also extremely effective. Especially if you are a man.

All right. Got my excuse, got my handkerchief, and am heading for the door. Wait . . . I think I forgot something . . .

You can't love every job you have.

The summer I was sixteen, I applied for a job at the new Six Flags Over Georgia. I wanted to work the Great American Scream Machine, or even the Log Ride. Instead, after a test and interview, they said, "We've given your talents a lot of thought and we've decided that you'll be sewing names on hats."

Makes you want to go right out and buy some mouse ears, doesn't it? Oh gosh, was that a bad job. I had to wear black double-knit pants, a black-and-white smock, and black loafers. These were the kind of clothes that if you offered someone the shirt off your back, they wouldn't take it. Still, it was a better job than the kind for which you don't need a shirt at all. (Tar. Five dollars an hour. Don't forget.) However, since the primary reason for having an amusement park job when you're sixteen is to buy gas for your car so you're able to date, and, if you're smart and lucky, to meet those dates at the park, I knew right away I would be my own worst enemy. I just couldn't imagine girls leaving Six Flags with stars in their eyes, going, "Did you see the guy in the smock in the hat booth? Oh my God!"

Sewing names was embarrassing, but at $1.65 an hour the pay was good. Besides, there were even more humiliating jobs. One was working the Flying Jenny, which was just some damn mule walking around in a circle for the kids who were scared of everything else. The boredom factor must have been out of this world, unless, of course, you made friends with Jenny. Then, a little hay, a little conversation, and who knows what could happen?

Sewing was also difficult. The machine was a table with a long handle on a swivel underneath. We had to practice for a month before the park opened. They gave us big black pieces of cloth and pink thread—which did not help the insecurities that went with the sewing machine—and a chart with the one hundred "Most Common Names." John, David, and Mary might seem simpler than Brandon, Jordan, Emmett, and Brittany, but they were all tough to stitch.

When the park finally opened for Sneak-a-Peek Weekend, there I was with my clean smock and double-knit black pants. I had my hundred names down so cold that *you* could do them in your sleep. My first customer was a guy and his wife and their daughter. He bought a sailor hat for the little girl. I said, "Would you like her name on it, sir?"

"Yes."

"Her name is?"

He said, "Cajava."

I had not practiced Cajava. C-a-j-a-v-a: the first name I sewed on a hat. Cajava. Where is she now? I hope she still has the hat.

Oh, I hated that job. I *hated* that job. But I loved the money. My first paycheck was $24.32, after taxes. I took it, walked to my car, and thought, "How the hell am I gonna spend this much money in one week?" And the next week there would be twenty-four more big ones coming in. Whoo!!!

Years later I discovered that my wife, Gregg, had *also* worked at Six Flags Over Georgia that summer. (I don't recall meeting. Trust me, I would have remembered.) Her job was even more demeaning than mine. Gregg had to roll around the park on skates, with a broom and a dustpan, cleaning up. Most of the time it was just trash, but occasionally it was a Code Thirteen. Vomit.

Eventually, Gregg and her sister and her cousin (who also worked there) got jobs in the Crystal Pistol, which was the song-and-dance review show. The only reason you went inside was to escape the stifling Georgia August heat. Gregg's ex-husband *sang* in the show, which I've always considered the only less-masculine job there than mine. I've only seen three pictures of the guy, and in every one he's got one hand on the piano and the other one lifted in the air. His mouth is open. Any time Gregg gives me grief about what I do, I just go, "Now here's a salute to those great American railroads! Let me get my hat!"

By the way, Twilley also worked at Six Flags. They put him in the candy shop. It was hardly a prestigious position but, of course, Twilley managed to have sex with a coworker. Seems he had to give her a ride home, and they wound up naked on her pool table.

I quit Six Flags before summer ended. Working at Six Flags was a lot like going to the state fair: You could see lots of body hair and always spot a family that made you feel very good about your own. Still, I'm sometimes nostalgic about my time there. Or maybe it's because somehow the words to the park-closing announcement are indelibly etched into my brain cells and I'm mistaking that for sentimentality.

"Ladies and gentlemen, the hour for closing has now arrived and we must say goodnight. Our hosts and hostesses hope you've enjoyed your stay and will come back to visit us soon. The park will reopen tomorrow morning at 10 A.M., but for now a pleasant goodnight."

Slam!—went the door on the hat booth, and I was gone.

Some jobs require you to work alone, but I've always been a people person. Besides, you don't get tips when you work by yourself.

After Six Flags, I took a job as a bellhop at the Sheraton Emory Hotel, right by Emory University and Emory Hospital. We were also across the street from the Centers for Disease Control, which always made me nervous. Part of my job was to change the letters on the sign out front—WELCOME LIONS CLUB—and I'd always hold my breath because I knew some strange things were going on at the CDC.

I learned fascinating bellhop tricks on the job that you might watch for the next time you check in. As I picked up someone's bag, I'd sneak a peek at their name tag to see where they came from. Then as I walked them to their room, I said, "And where did y'all come in from? Seattle? Oh God, I love Seattle. My brother lives in Seattle and he just says it's the best place in the whole world."

The bellhop's life was great preparation for a life of making a fool of myself onstage, though now it's for a lot more money. But back then, I knew that if I could get a hotel guest talking to me, I'd get tipped. Sometimes I could hear the hand in the pocket go from rolling change to grabbing actual folding money.

I also quit that job—surprised?—but soon returned to the hotel as a maintenance man. It wasn't such hard work, since the place was falling apart and there was no stopping it. The hotel also didn't have enough heat in the winter or near enough air-conditioning in the summer.

I worked for Craig Todd. He was funny and decent and he taught me the joyous art of screwing off at work. Once, just for fun, we cut the heads off three thousand books of hotel matches, and stuffed them in a copper tube that we'd crimped one end of in the workroom vise. Then we crimped the other end almost shut, got a coat hanger, made a launching pad, and trailed a fuse of match heads across the back parking lot. While Craig and I sat there arguing about whether or not our little rocket would work, we noticed guests curiously looking on, wondering if we were some sort of free entertainment. They're probably still complaining that there was no champagne buffet.

We lit the fuse and hid behind somebody's car. That thing took off and I swear it has not yet come down. Somewhere a projectile crashed through someone's roof and they're still wondering if was part of a secret government rocket, or if miniature extraterrestrials had invaded their home. In the South it could be either, you know.

As a public service, there's another hotel secret I feel I should reveal, if only to redeem myself for playing with match heads and probably causing three weeks of alien invader headlines in the *National Enquirer*.

In the summer guests would constantly call to complain that their air-conditioning wasn't strong enough. Frankly, there was nothing at all we could do about it. The central unit was old and the hotel owner wasn't going to put any more money into it. So Craig taught me a work-around. He said to always carry a small screwdriver with a pocket-clip on it. Then, when I got an air-conditioning complaint, to walk into the room and say, "Whoo, boy, this isn't right." Next, remove the thermostat cover, stick the screwdriver in, twist it back and forth, and pretend to adjust it. As I did that, I should put my hand in front of the vent, tweak, test, tweak, test. Then motion to the guest. "Come over here. Does that feel better? Tell me when it gets good." They'll put their hand up and finally go, "Right there, right there."

It always worked. I'd leave with a nice tip, they'd be smiling, and I hadn't done a damn thing except perfect the art of bull-shitting.

When my friend Jim Kumpe quit his job at Kroger's deli he recommended me for the position based on the fine work I'd done for the Sheraton Emory. He went to Europe and left me to slice ham and bologna. That job drew down $7.00 an hour and I thought I was rich.

Say what you want about slicing bologna, the grocery store is still a great, great place to meet women. The aisles were always well stocked and many young ladies who passed through regularly were either single or not happily married. Slice their bologna right and anything could happen. I was so shameless in my pursuit that more than once the managers pulled me into the office for a lecture about "fishing off Kroger's dock." And to think of all that time I wasted fishing with Burns and Chastain.

Kroger turned out to be about more than meeting women. That's where I first learned how to handle a microphone and discovered that I liked it. One day the boss asked if anyone was interested in doing the sales announcements for the store. I said, "Yeah, I'll do it!" I had to read them into a tape recorder. They'd play every fifteen or twenty minutes all day long, over the public address system.

Soon, the whole town could hear me saying, "Attention, Kroger shoppers. In our deli today we feature Virginia baked ham. Regularly three-eighty-nine a pound, this week only two-nineteen. Also, try some delicious mustard potato salad. Regularly a dollar-nine, this week only seventy-nine-cents a pint."

Slowly, I learned to work the grocery store crowd and make them excited about being out shopping. I was good at it. Soon, any time the store had a spot announcement, I was the guy. <click> "Clean up on aisle five. Broken glass on aisle five." <click>

These announcements made me a celebrity, especially to my family. They shopped at Kroger and they'd hang around just to hear me say things like, "Attention Kroger shoppers. Visit the meat counter and find out about our boneless ham shank special." My family would find me in the store and say, "Just heard you doing the thing about the ham. Nice work."

You know, it just doesn't get any better.

Not only did I work for a living, I also went to school at Georgia Tech. I won't go on about it except to say that after three years they asked me not to return. I wasn't a discipline problem. I'd committed no crimes. Burns and I hadn't flashed BAs anywhere on campus. I simply felt out of place and my grades reflected it. Though I'd done very well in high school, college was a tough adjustment. I'd gone from a small town and a small school where I was one of the two top dogs to being a face in the crowd. I wasn't involved in any campus social life. Nobody knew me. I didn't fit in. I didn't study because I took courses that didn't interest me. My major was industrial management. You can imagine me in a suit and tie, behind a desk, right? The only reason I went to Tech was that it was the closest school to home. I suppose I planned to prepare for a life doing what my dad had done. But I couldn't work up any enthusiasm for the allure of corporate life.

Those were my lost years. However, I've since been acknowledged as a Distinguished Alumni by my alma mater.

Thank you very much.

After I left Georgia Tech (and Kroger), I hung out a lot at my father's farm. I grew a full beard and my hair went past my shoulders. I drew and painted and worked lights for a friend's rock and roll band. In other words, I was going broke in a hurry. Through some back channels my dad finally had some friends call and tell me there were a few job openings at IBM, and maybe I ought to apply.

I decided to take the plunge. When I went down there, every guy waiting for an interview looked like a Harvard graduate. I looked like I'd just swept up the office. When it was my turn, the man in personnel said, "If we hired you, would you get rid of all of this hair?"

"Yeah, if you hire me," I said. "But I'm not getting rid of it for the interview."

He said, "Tell me good stuff about you." So I talked and talked and talked. Then he said, "Tell me something bad about you."

I said, "Man, I'm trying to sell you a product. I'm not going to tell you what's wrong with it." He laughed and I got the job. I was nineteen or twenty. I worked in the Atlanta office, in dispatch. My first assignment was to take calls from customers who had broken machines.

"IBM dispatch. May I have your area code and phone number please? What machine are you having a problem with? And the nature of your problem? All right, sir, I'll have a representative get it touch with you as soon as possible."

Like all other IBM employees, I had to conform to the dress code. I think even the janitors had to wear suits and ties. So I went right out and got a couple of $40 suits and some awful shirts. Then I went into my dad's attic and pulled out his old wingtips—we wear the same size—and polished them to look like new. Then I fit right in. Just like Joe Luckie.

Joe Luckie—isn't that the greatest name of all time?—worked right across the hall in parts. Joe came from New York. For his first two years Joe wore only two suits. He only *owned* two suits: one blue and one brown. He'd wear the blue one Monday, Wednesday, and Friday, the brown one Tuesday and Thursday. The following week he'd alternate it, just to mix it up. Finally, after a couple of years, his parents sent him a gray suit for Christmas.

IBM's office occupied the fourteenth floor of a high-rise in Atlanta's Colony Square. One morning before work, Joe and I bought coffee and doughnuts in the central shopping area downstairs. Afterward, we got on the elevator for the ride up to the office. We stopped on the sixth floor and a guy got on that neither of us had ever seen before. He was just another of the thousands who worked in the high-rise.

When the door closed the guy looked right at Joe and did a double take. Then he said, "Hey, you got a new suit!"

That's when Joe suddenly realized that everyone in the building knew he *only* had two suits. I tried to keep from falling down, laughing. Joe worked to contain his embarrassment.

Isn't it nice that there's always someone around to make you feel better about yourself?

The ideal job is one in which you like what you do. The next best thing is one in which you can have fun. The great thing about IBM was that even before I considered doing stand-up, I got to hone my comedic skills and have more fun than shooting fish in a barrel.

After I'd been at the company a while, they promoted me at dispatch. Now I worked in a "quad" with Dwight Stanton, Jesse Frank, and Cynthia Sloane. We no longer took customer calls. We assigned work to servicemen instead. We did really well, always scoring at the top of the performance charts and getting tons of work done. Even so, we were so terribly bored that the only way to avoid devolving right on the spot was to play practical jokes. For instance, each of the servicemen had his own radio number. They'd all call in every day with the same routine. For example:

"Hello, this is Lester Nobby, 509." Lester had a distinctive voice that reflected his religious and straightforward nature. He was always pleasant but always all business.

We quickly learned to imitate the servicemen. Then we would pretend to go to the bathroom, run around the corner, call our quad, and try to fool the other guys. One day Dwight Stanton announced that nature had called. He turned the corner and, sure enough, three seconds later the phone rang. Jesse and I looked at each other with the same thought: "Dwight's trying to get us."

Jesse picked up and heard, "This is Lester Nobby, 509." He motioned to me and I grabbed an extension.

Jesse said, "Lester, you ole sonofabitch, what the hell are you up to?"

Nobby was aghast. "What the . . . ?" he said.

"The hell you say, Lester," Jesse added.

Suddenly Dwight walked around the corner. Our mouths dropped open and we did the mature thing and hung up. Then Lester called back.

"What the heck's going on up there?" Lester demanded hotly.

"What are you talking about, Lester?" I said.

"Well, I just called up there and got cussed out."

"You didn't call here, Lester. We've been sitting here all day." (If you're reading this, Lester, sorry.)

Another stunt we pulled to relieve our boredom was to send guys on temporary assignments. That meant they had to take a different job or territory for a few days. My favorite victim was a guy named Clay Felton. Felton was a legend because he was only twenty-seven and three times divorced. He also played softball fanatically. This one weekend we knew he had a statewide-level game scheduled. So on the Thursday before the game we decided to send Felton on temporary assignment.

First we left him a message to call "Jerry Duncan" at headquarters.

"What the hell's that all about?" said Felton, when he checked in with me.

"I don't know," I said.

Since the servicemen always called in from phone booths, I offered to connect him to Duncan.

"Yeah, if you don't mind."

"Sure, no problem." I put him on hold and then said to my quadmates, "I've got Felton on the line. Cynthia, you're Jerry Duncan's secretary." Then, back to Felton, "Okay, hold on, Clay. Talk to you later, buddy." Then Cynthia picked up the phone.

"Jerry Duncan's office."

"Yes, this is Clay Felton returning Jerry's call."

"He's on another line, could you hold one minute please?" A minute later, I came on as Duncan.

"Jerry Duncan."

"Yessir, this is Clay Felton, I had a message from you."

"John, glad you called me back. We've got a secret installation going on at NASA this weekend. We're pulling about twenty guys from throughout the country and you've been selected as one of those going."

"This weekend?"

"Yes, Clay, and I have to tell you: This is going to look extremely good on your resume."

"When would I have to leave?" Felton asked, clearly unhappy.

"Well, we need you to leave right away, Clay. God, we've got over one hundred and fifty 420s to install."

"I've got to call my wife," said Felton, looking for any way out.

"Clay, we'd ask that you not call your wife, it's top secret."

"Okay, sir. Thank you," said Felton. Then he hung up, defeated. We laughed for a good five minutes, then beeped Felton. When he called back I said, "Felton, listen, by the way: Do you recognize this voice? 'Jerry Duncan, headquarters.' "

All we heard on the other end was a scream and the words, "You sonsabitches!"

Yes, working for a big corporation was more fun than I'd expected. The servicemen never knew what hit them. I did one of my favorite tricks whenever a guy named Mike Lewis called in. He was way too upbeat.

"Hey, Jeff! This is Mike Lewis! What's going on!"

I'd go, "Hey, Mike, listen, you gotta call . . . ufacturing . . . and what . . . going . . . and they need . . . 3-8 . . . 0-2."

"Jeff, you're breaking up."

"Mi . . . go . . ."

"You're breaking up, I'll call you back." Then he'd hang up. Since he was in a phone booth, I'd think, "There's one quarter." Then he'd call back. I'd say, "IBM dispatch."

"Hey, Jeff! It's Mike! Man, God, that was weird! You were breaking up like crazy!"

"IBM dispatch."

"Yeah, Jeff, it's me, Mike!"

"Hello? IBM dispatch?"

"Jeff, it's me, Mike!"

"Hello? Hey, if you're there, call me back." There's two quarters. Then Mike would call back again.

"Hey, Jeff, it's me, Mike! Something wrong with the phones up there?"

"I don't know, Mike, we've been having problems with them all day long. It started . . . ," and I'd just cut the line dead. There's three quarters.

Now you know why it took so long to get IBM's machines fixed. The servicemen usually spent all day in a phone booth just trying to get their assignments. Do you think we were at all responsible for the big layoffs at Big Blue? Nah.

We didn't limit our practical jokes to the men in the field.

The main receptionist used to drive us bonkers because she was so stupid. She'd always disconnect us, or connect us to the wrong place, or cut our callers off altogether. (Come to think of it now, maybe she was just giving us a taste of our own medicine!) It got so we hated her and we made it our mission for a month just to mess with her.

Once we had Joe Luckie linger in the lobby and watch her. Then Jesse called the receptionist and said, "This is Jim Johnson with the telephone company. We have a reported problem with 555-6200."

The receptionist said, "Yes, I have been having problems with this line."

"What we're gonna do," said Jesse/Jim, "is have a gentlemen working on that line for about the next five minutes or so, so we'd ask that if it *does* ring, *please* don't answer it because we're send-ing a burst of power across the lines. If you pick up, the electricity could severely injure the phone repairman.''

The phones were set up so that if no one answered after about three rings at the receptionist's station, the lines would roll over down the hall to the secondary receptionists. We waited about sixty seconds and called the main receptionist. Joe Luckie, our lookout, later said that the woman just sat there staring at the phone as it rang. No way she would answer it. Suddenly, he said, her eyes got as big as saucers and she jumped up from her desk and took off running down the hall.

''DON'T ANSWER THE PHONE! DON'T ANSWER THE PHONE!'' she yelled. But the call rolled over, someone answered it, and Hillary screamed. ''ARRRGGGGHHHHH!!!''

Next thing we knew the receptionist was in the break room with a cold washcloth on her head, saying, ''You killed the phone man! You killed the phone man!''

Another time, again posing as repairmen, we told her to put her entire phone console into the trash can because we were going to blow the dust out of the lines and we didn't want her to get dirt all over her desk. And she did it.

I worked in dispatch for a year, but I could tell there wasn't much room for career growth. Fortunately, the company held aptitude testing and I signed up on the chance that I might get a better position. When the results came back, they said, ''You have an aptitude for sewing names on hats.'' Just kidding. They wanted me to become a serviceman and fix machines. I just had to go to the IBM school.

ARRRGGGHHH!

I guess I deserved it. The weird thing was that if I opted to go to school and didn't pass, I couldn't go back to dispatch. I'd lose my job and I'd *really* have to sew hats, or worse, work with tar.

Though naturally pragmatic, as you know, I took the leap and went to school. I passed. My big reward was a transfer to Sarasota, Florida.

I was the youngest guy at that backwater office and got to handle every crappy assignment. If three calls came in—two blocks away, four blocks away, and 185 miles away, I got to take the long drive in my Volkswagen Beetle with no air-conditioning and no radio.

Of course, whenever I had to call dispatch, my old friends tried to mess around with me. I didn't mind. Even if I was the junior repairman, I was at least out on the road and my quadmates were still in the office.

Okay, there was a downside. Because it was a suboffice, I often went on calls to repair machines *about which I knew nothing.* In retrospect, this was also good comedy training. I had to walk into a strange place and pull it off. Sometimes I'd stand there, with my arm resting on a big metal something, and say, "So, where's the machine?"

They'd go, "You're leaning on it."

"Oh yeah," I said, acting like I knew what I was doing. "This baby here." I had to read manuals to learn how to take the *covers* off some machines. But I learned that if the customer liked me, I could buy a little time. It was just like making hotel guests like me for tips. Then I'd fix what I could and for the rest I'd scream for help. Mostly, on pure instinct, I did okay.

IBM was a good employer and I wanted to do well on the job, no matter how many practical jokes I orchestrated. My dad had helped me get on board and I wanted to make him proud. In fact, I pretty much wore my cheap suits into the ground doing so. Then one day I found a really good deal—$89—for a gray wool suit. (Maybe because I bought it in June?) I bought it because, based on my performance in dispatch, the company had invited me to one of those breakfast-with-the-president functions.

I decided I would introduce myself to the bigwigs and let them know exactly who Jeff Foxworthy was. And that's just what I did, very confidently. Afterward, as I stood in a corner, drinking my little good-morning orange juice, a guy I worked with came up and whispered in my ear: "Hey, Fox, check out your pants." Not only were they unzipped, they gapped open wide enough to fly a Frisbee through. I was mortified. Meet the president then zip your pants. I looked over at the higher-ups, standing by the podium. I knew what they were saying.

"Did you see that goofy Foxworthy kid with his pants un-zipped?"

Hey, at least they remembered me. What more could an enter-tainer want?

Roommates and Their Habitats

Sooner or later, we all have a
roommate. Parents and siblings don't count because they're just
part of the deal—unless they come to live with you when you're
an adult. Then, they'll call themselves houseguests. After a couple
of days you want to call them anything you can get away with,
including a taxi. With our spouses, we *supposedly* had a choice
about being together, though I'm certain many of us don't remember it that way. Don't even get me started on in-laws.

Roommates are tough. You've got to pick someone you can beat up on because you never get along with everybody always. Even if you shared an apartment with the Pope, I guarantee that three weeks into it you'd be going, "Hey, you mind picking up the cape, man? And quit leaving the papal miter on the kitchen counter."

I've always looked for a roommate with a sense of humor, someone roughly like me, only different. I'm not so sure living with myself is any piece of cake. You definitely don't want someone wilder than you are. You want the same degree of wildness. If you're the wild one you'll feel like you're living with your Aunt Florence. If your roommate is the wild one, *you'll* feel like Aunt Florence while he's holding a naked Twister Bingo session in his bedroom—or worse, in the living room, where you can see it all. You both need to stagger in side by side. The *Odd Couple* approach never works.

An ideal roommate has a horny sister. Or *is* someone's horny sister. Or is one and has one. Or knows one. I'm not just kidding around here.

Paying the rent on time is also a good quality.

One person to absolutely avoid as a roommate is an ex-wife, no matter what sick circumstances drive you to again share the same living space. First, you don't want to be around when she's getting phone calls from other guys. Second, she doesn't want to be around while you're burning her clothes.

No matter how you fare during these days of swine and losers, I promise that you will soon miss the times when you were wild and free and living with someone you could just move out on at any time. Maybe for no other reason than that I'm a sentimental guy, about five years ago I got nostalgic for the apartment life. Then Gregg got pregnant. She ate all my food and threw up once a day. It was just like having a roommate all over again.

When I first left home, I got lucky and lived for a while with my dad. You can just imagine the fun we had.

Big Jim lived on Atlanta's north side. He drank, threw parties, smoked, and cussed. Yeah, Big Jim was pretty cool to have as a father. When I was still in high school I'd try to spend the weekends at his condo. I had a car and I'd drive to Big Jim's Friday evening with my girlfriend.

Jim would say, "Hey, you kids wanna spend the night?" Music to a teenager in heat. I'd say sure. Then my stepmother would call my girlfriend's mother and go, "Is it okay if the kids spend the night?"

Did I already say he was cool to have as a dad? Now you know why I moved in with him as soon as I could.

When I couldn't stay at the condo legitimately, because he was at the farm, I'd sneak over—again, with a girlfriend. But I didn't want Big Jim to know. I was so meticulous in covering my tracks that I'd even measure how high the window blinds were off the sill so I could put them back in exactly the right place.

"Okay, I think it was an inch and a half below the middle of the window."

"Are you sure," my girlfriend would say?

"Get dressed and then get me a ruler, okay?"

It would take me an hour to get the house right.

Ten years later, for reasons that still elude me, I confessed all this to Big Jim. "But I bet you never knew I went over to the condo."

"Of course I did," he said. "You went there every weekend when I was gone."

Kids. We think we're so smart. Parents know everything because they've usually done *everything* themselves. Then Big Jim continued, "I'd always come back and go, 'That little bastard's been here screwing.' "

"You should have told me you knew," I said, as I tried to keep my composure.

"Why?" he asked.

"You could have saved me a lot of time cleaning that I could have spent doing, uh . . . other things."

"That's why I didn't say anything. I even had to let the maid go because you did such a good job."

But if Big Jim did me a favor by letting me use the condo—though he was clearly well compensated—I took care of him, too. For instance, sometimes Big Jim would say, "Look, you and I are going out and having a few drinks tonight."

I'd say, "Daddy, I can't. I've got a date."

"Well, I know that," he'd say, "But if anybody asks, you and I are going out for a few drinks tonight. Okay?"

"Okay. Where did we go?"

Nothing like covering for your dad.

Once he called me, excited and upset, and said, "I've locked my keys in my car."

"Where are you?"

"I'm at the bar at the end of the street."

"At the end of *your* street?" Big Jim wasn't married to my mom at the time, but he *was* married. So I delivered his keys and found him drinking with his secretary.

"Dad," I said. "I'm eighteen years old, and even *I* know to get farther away from the house, for God's sake. If you're going to fool around, at least get out of the sight line of the kitchen!"

Big Jim took risks on his own, but he wasn't about to let me be an idiot. When I lived with him he had a rule that when I went out I should always call him if I was, say, too drunk to drive and didn't plan to come home that evening. I respected him and called when the situation arose. But once it got to be four in the morning, I was plastered, and I was scared to death to call. I decided I had to drive home, but my friend Eddie wouldn't let me. (He was right.) I said, "I ain't calling home at four in the morning and waking up Big Jim. I'll take my chances."

Eddie said, "I ain't letting you in the car. I'll call him." We went to Eddie's apartment. I lay down on the sofa and Eddie called my dad. I could only hear his end of the conversation.

"Mr. Foxworthy? This is Eddie Harlen? I'm fine, how are you? Oh, good, yeah, school's going all right. Yeah, yeah, I'm still going out with her. Anyway, I just called to say that Jeff's had one too many and he's gonna be sleeping on my couch tonight. Oh, I appreciate it. I surely will. Okay, bye." He hung up the phone and I was speechless. Finally, I said, "He didn't get mad?"

Eddie said, "Nope. In fact, he just came in the house five minutes ago himself."

After my dad moved to Tampa I shared an apartment with my sister, Jennifer. Poor Jennifer. The only thing worse than being a Redneck is having a Redneck brother.

We were pretty pathetic.

The needle on our record player was so worn out that we had to pile spare change on the arm to make it work at all. It started with a penny, then a penny and a dime, then a nickel, then all three. By the time we got to a dollar twenty five it was time to break down and get a new needle. But at least we'd saved enough money.

I also seemed to collect food. By the time I married Gregg, I had refrigerator items that had lived with me in eight different apartments. I just couldn't throw them out. We'd been through too much together. I've still got a jar of olives that's been with me since the beginning. I just don't think it's fair to move to the nice house with the subzero refrigerator and throw away stuff that's stuck with me as long as it took me to make something of myself. I figured the olives should live the good life, too.

Jennifer and I belonged to the Utility of the Month Club. You don't really want to be a member. That's when something different is shut off each month. This always seemed to happen when my dad came up to visit to check on how we were doing. I remember the phone being cut off and having to drive to the 7-Eleven to make calls. The next month it was the electricity. I made my sister go down to the department of water and power and tell them our aunt lived with us, and that she was on a dialysis machine, so they would they *please* turn it back on.

They did.

Eventually we got all the utilities running at the same time. That's when General Motors Acceptance Corporation tried to repossess my wheels. I worked at IBM and I had to have a two-tone Rally Sport Camaro. Big Jim had said that if I got enough for a down payment, he'd match it. I saved the money and after a series of "walk away" negotiations—Big Jim did the walking while I drove my friends past the car lot and pointed to the Camaro behind the fence and said, "There's my car!"—I got it. It had close to $1,000 worth of stereo equipment, including an equalizer and a power booster. Even at minimum volume it would make the windows shake.

But I was behind in the payments. One night the GMAC guy showed up at the door about 6:00 P.M.

He said, "Mr. Foxworthy, I'm from GMAC. I've come to get your car. You haven't made a payment in three months. Unless you can give me $500 right now, the car's going with me."

I said, "500 bucks? Who keeps that kind of cash on them?"

He said, "Can't you write me a check?"

"A check? Hell . . . *yeah*, I can write you a check! I thought you needed money." So I wrote him a bad check and hid the car in a friend's garage until I got caught up on my payments. I couldn't believe he took the check. I was tempted to pay the *whole* thing off right there. Maybe even say, "Tell you what, here's $500 extra. Go get your wife something nice."

I'm gonna be a congressman when I grow up.

Eventually my sister and I *did* break up, but not because we'd lost interest in each other. Nope. It was because of Bear.

Bear was a little white poodle—as you know, one of my least favorite dogs—that Jennifer insisted on having in the apartment.

Bear always crapped on the floor. Jennifer and I worked all the time, and often stayed out all night, so it wasn't really Bear's fault that no one was around to walk him. Thank goodness he only weighed four pounds. It was relatively simple to clean up after him. But it was nonetheless a nuisance.

One night I finally decided I'd had enough of Bear. I decided to make my sister pay for bringing him to live with us.

It was Halloween. While we were out "trick or treating," Bear had again relieved himself in the apartment. I came home first and could smell it but could not find it. I searched for half an hour, then gave up and plotted my revenge. I took a big Tootsie Roll out of my candy bag and as I watched TV and wondered where the dog had buried his treasure, I kneaded the Tootsie Roll into a familiar shape. (Remember, I'm good at this.) I put a little bend on it and a little taper on one end, and then I put it on the floor next to the couch.

I waited until Jennifer came in. She went straight to the refrigerator for a Coke. She lit a cigarette. When she walked into the living room, her nose crinkled at the smell and I said, "Oh God, Bear messed on the floor again!"

"I'm sorry," she said.

"Don't be sorry," I said. "Just help me *find* it. I can't even find it. I'm gettin' so SICK of this."

"Okay, okay," she said. "I'll help you look."

She got down on her hands and knees and started searching. I pretended to look around, too. Suddenly I said, "Here it is."

"I'll get a paper towel," she said.

"Don't bother," I replied. I double-checked to make sure it was *my* little creation, then I popped it into my mouth.

Jennifer dropped her Coke and ran to the bathroom. The sounds she made let me know that my mission had been accomplished.

Bear moved the next day. So did I.

Only in Georgia can you share an apartment with your sister

and later get away with an explanation like, "Yeah, but we broke up for the sake of the dog. . . ."

There's a reason for clichés like, "You don't know what you've got until it's gone." After my sister and I split up, I moved to Florida and I couldn't find another place for four months. I had to sleep on the foldout couch of a guy I worked with at IBM. Ralph Hubbard was forty-eight, wore two hearing aids, and let me keep my clothes in a suitcase in the hall. He was actually a great guy, but we couldn't go on living like that. Then somebody told me that Stanley Cobb had a great place on the beach in Sarasota and wanted a roommate.

If I thought living with Hubbard was odd, Cobb beat it by a mile. He was a bullshit artist deluxe. Every month Stanley would say, "Just write a check to me for the rent and the utilities, and I'll pay for everything." Six months later I came home and found an eviction notice on the door. He hadn't paid the rent for nine months. That was a Friday night. The notice said that we had until Monday morning to be gone, or the marshals would throw us and everything we owned out on the street. I sat on the living room couch and tried to figure out what to do next. That's when Cobb called. I made things worse when I lost my temper and threatened to beat his ass. Now he wouldn't even come home. Then all these other people started calling, saying, "Hey, he owes me 800 bucks, that bastard."

Then it struck me. I said, "Really? Come on over!"

Stanley has a really nice TV, probably valued at close to eight hundred bucks. I'm going to be in the bathroom brushing my hair. The door's open."

All weekend long I let people come in and take his stuff.

It was my first and last rummage sale.

I figured my luck could only improve, and I was right.

My next roommate was named Dexter McDougal. Everybody called him Dex. I met Dex when I dated his sister, but he and I ended up hitting it off better than she and I. Pretty soon we moved in together. (Dex's sister even spent the night from time to time.)

I consider my place with Dex my first singles apartment. Singles apartments are the same all over the country, aren't they?

Let's walk through the place room by room and I'll show you the highlights of fine Southern, twentysomething living.

The apartment had two bedrooms, each with a bathroom. Also, a little hall, a kitchen, a dining room, and a living room.

In the living room we had the telephone wire spool for the coffee table. Saw it sitting off the side of a road, borrowed a pickup truck, and hauled it home. Some people shellac them, others like the natural pitted, tar-smeared look. We painted ours with the only colors we could find in Dex's dad's garage: aqua and black. That went really well with the green-gold shag carpet and the orange sofa. The spool top was always cluttered with the remains of a wild Saturday night, usually from three months earlier.

We were lucky to have the sofa. We also found it on the street. I remember cruising by, seeing it balanced on the curb, and thinking, "Heeyyyyy. If that baby's there after dark, she'll be in my living room before midnight." We also had a bean bag chair covered with duct tape to keep the "beans" from falling out and the material from simply disintegrating.

Our place had the same green-gold shag rug that you find in apartments everywhere. I'm certain that there's one manufacturer who carpets every apartment nationwide, and that it's part of a government conspiracy, and the real reason for our staggering national debt. This carpet turned up naturally at the corners and smelled like someone had soaked it in spilled milk, Jack Daniels, and cat pee. This was when it was new. When one of Dex's friends parked his motorcycle on our living room carpet, we got an oil stain as a bonus. Within months, we'd tramped down the rug by the front door so much that we couldn't even rake it back up. Every time we'd try, we'd kick up a rabbit.

Of course we had the cinder blocks and boards shelving. We finally painted them black to give then a nice look. The stereo was really just an old receiver I'd bought for eight bucks at a garage sale. All the panel lights were burned out so you could never tell which station you were listening to. Our TV was a plastic Ford Philco model. Ford has always been known for making a damn good television, right? The transmission broke in it a couple of times, but what the hell, this was in precable days—we had the aluminum foil antenna—and there wasn't much to watch anyway. I think it was a color set. Well, kinda color.

I had a deer head on the living room wall. He sported a baseball cap, sunglasses, and a cigarette. He looked like he'd been shot while walking in the parade at Mardi Gras. Something that nice you *have* to show off.

I don't think we owned anything framed. Everything was stuck to the walls with tape or thumb tacks. We had posters of different things like cars, women, and rock and roll singers. The important things in life. We also had a lava lamp in the living room, but it didn't work. The light would go on but it was otherwise impotent. The lava would just sit there and never go up.

Our bedrooms were your basic pigstyes. Dex's mattress sat on the floor, mine on a box spring without a frame. Clearly, I had the deluxe accommodations. Both were protected by huge piles of clothes, some dirty and some clean. It was always tough to tell the difference, although we did the laundry every month at Dex's parents' house.

My bedroom had milk crates for nightstands. Also, my collection of stolen road signs. Dex's bedroom had an ironing board that he used for bookshelves. One of my brother's friends said he made it with a girl on that ironing board during a party. We're still not sure if we believe that. Both rooms also featured the hippest in bedroom decor: blankets for curtains, old pizza boxes, and drinking glasses growing new forms of life.

A small hallway with a mystery stain on the carpet and a Budweiser mirror on the wall connected the bedrooms and there was a balcony off the back. We were on the top floor of a two-story building. Location is, of course, everything, as I'm sure the couple who lived below us soon realized. They were both in their eighties and retired. I'm sure they learned some stuff in their golden years. Occasionally we'd hear them holler things at Dex like, "Don't let him bring your sister over again!"

The balcony had a rusted-out hibachi grill, and an old towel in the corner that you wouldn't have touched even with a stick. If you did, you'd have had to register at the Centers for Disease Control. The towel had been rained on and was covered with spider webs. It was also as stiff as petrified wood. I'd always meant to string some yellow police barrier tape around it, but I never found the time. We also had a bike with no chain on the balcony and plants that we moved out there when the leaves finally fell off, leaving only sticks and dirt.

The dining room was empty except for another bicycle and some old bags of trash we never took out.

The kitchen was tiny. The drawers held two forks, two spoons, and a turkey baster. (You figure it out. I can't.) We used the stove to light cigarettes. The refrigerator had a couple of beers, some junk food, and my olives. We had a can of she-crab soup in the pantry, though I don't know why. Neither Dex nor I was ever hungry enough to eat it. When we did eat, we would leave the dishes in the sink until there were none left in the cabinet. Then Dex would talk his mother into coming over and washing them. Somehow he'd also get her to clean up the place.

Both our bathrooms made the local Shell station restrooms look immaculate. We even posted signs reading "For customer use only" but it didn't help. We had shower curtains no one could approach without a radiation suit. Plus, there was never enough toilet paper. Occasionally I'd steal a roll from IBM. (See, a lot of those Redneck jokes are firsthand.) Dex would let it run out then he'd use the cardboard rolls it came on or duckwalk to the kitchen and get a paper towel before he'd break down and buy a new package of TP. More likely, he'd steal it from some public restroom.

The saddest part of all this is that we actually brought women there!

You might think our living conditions were awful, but it's all relative, just like fame. We had a friend eating out of a hubcap, so we felt pretty good about ourselves. Still, it's no wonder why singles apartments are about as close as we all come to being homeless.

The only good thing about a singles apartment is that you never *really* had to get your roommate's mother to clean it up. At least not until the day you moved and tried to get the security deposit back. Then you'd argue with the landlord.

"No sir, the back door was missing when we moved in here. The pizzas were always on the ceiling."

As you get older, if you still live the apartment life, you find you have to tidy up occasionally. Or you have to at least try to make people think you do. We've all done that, been home on the weekend, had the phone ring: "Hey, we're in the neighborhood, thought we'd stop by and see y'all."

You always say, "Sure, come on, we'd love to have you." You hang up and do that flight of the bumblebee. Ninety miles an hour, fluff and stuff. You're sweating when they get there, and the first thing you always say is "Excuse the house, it's a mess. Y'all come on in." Why don't we just tell them the truth? "Y'all, this is the cleanest our place has been in six years! Just don't open the closet, you'll kill yourselves."

This refusal to play by the commonsense rules of hygiene is one reason why single people throw the best parties: They don't have to worry about their furniture getting messed up. Their friends can destroy everything in the place. They're out fifteen bucks, so what?

Single people *do* throw the best parties, don't you think? There's always a good chance somebody's coming out of their clothes before the night's out. Most of the time it's the woman who's dancing by herself way too early in the evening. "It's only 7:15 and Peggy's dancing by herself. That shirt's coming off tonight, I guarantee you."

Single people don't consider it a good party unless the cops have been there at least a dozen times. When they arrive it's the same scenario every time: 400 drunks trying to act like they're not drunk. One guy is the spokesman for the group. "It's the cops, turn the stereo down! Put your shirt on, Peggy! Y'all be cool, let me do the talking. Welcome back, Officer Mitchell!!! Don't shoot!"

Then to the crowd: "I told him don't shoot!"

Then back to the cops. "I'm glad you're back, I wanna report a crime. Larry puked in the aquarium. Stinks very much bad in here. Hey listen, if I lie down on the sidewalk will you draw my picture with that little chalk y'all have?"

No one ever went home from those parties. They just slept where they fell. When you'd get up the next day, it'd look like *Jonestown: The Morning After.* You'd try to wake up people you'd never met before. "Hey man-with-no-pants-and-a-fireman's-helmet-on, please get up, I've got to go to work. All right, lock the door when you leave. I just found a new sofa, and I don't want anything to happen to it."

I once went to toga party from which I walked home naked. Thank goodness it was only two blocks from the apartment. I'm still trying to figure out where I had the key. If you know, please don't tell me.

Throwing parties, like everything in life, adheres to the principle of the Great Circle. I used to be the king of throwing a big blast. Then, the first time I realized I had gotten older was when I worked in Daytona Beach one year during spring break. I found myself at three in the morning standing on my hotel balcony in my boxer shorts, screaming, "Go to bed! Go . . . to . . . bed! People are trying to sleep!" Then I walked inside, threw myself back into bed, and realized I had become an old man.

Dex worked the three-to-eleven shift at the Sarasota Hospital, monitoring machines in the intensive care unit. He would often get bored and call home, and I would relay the baseball game to him over the phone.

"Here's the wind, the stretch. Low and outside, ball three."

Then Dex would say, "Ah crap, somebody just straightlined."

"Okay, I'll let you go."

"Nah, just one more pitch," he'd say. That was pretty much Dex's attitude toward life. And death.

During the summer, Dex got an even better job. He worked in a mental institution and had to show up every morning in the smoking room to light the patients' cigarettes. For some reason, they wouldn't allow them to use their own matches.

Dex told me about one guy in the institution named Art. He said when he first met Art he had no idea why Art was in the mental institution. Dex would light Art's cigarette, then Art would sit there and say, "Hey, did you see that Cubs game last night? Man, that was something else. Cubs score three in the second, they come back, the Reds get four in the fifth." He said Art was as normal as anybody he'd ever met until his cigarette got down to the last couple of puffs. Then suddenly Art would start shaking like a dog passing a pinecone and would spew the most vile and common curse words. Then he'd reach in his pack, pull out a new cigarette and light it with the burned-down butt, take a drag off it and, as if nothing had happened, go, "So anyway, in the eighth, Sandburg comes back with a two-run homer . . ."

Dex and I were not only pigs about how we lived. The word sometimes described our personalities, too.

We called our apartment the Penile Palace, ''where every night
is Ladies Night. Thursday night is Titty Night. Bring one, get the
other one in absolutely free!'' I'm sure it was this enthusiasm for
women, and not grievous errors in our upbringing, that led to Dex
and me to stage monthly contests based on our conquests of
women.

Isn't it great what you can get away with when you don't live
at home?

We had a chart in the kitchen, right over the phone, and an
honor system. We devised an intricate point system based solely
on our womanizing. You could get bonus points if you did it in the
bathtub. Even more points if the water got cold. We were extremely competitive, but invariably, at the end of every month we
would always be within four or five points of each other.

Sometimes Dex would be so close that he'd say things like, ''I
know this girl at work. I could beat you this month. I could call up
this girl and win.''

But he never could because I had an unbeatable threat. All I had
to do was say, ''Dex, don't make me call your sister.''

I think what scared him more than his sister being two quick
points—unless I also went for a bonus—was that afterward he
would have to hear all the details. That was part of the honor system. We had to identify the woman and describe exactly what had
happened. If nothing else, it was an important lesson in telling the
truth.

People ask me now if looking back I'm ashamed of this base
and degrading behavior. Of course . . . not.

You have to trust your roommates. But sometimes they take advantage of you just for the heck of it.

I had to be at IBM each morning at eight o'clock, wearing my suit and tie, to fix machines. Dex got home from the hospital each night at eleven-fifteen. Every night he'd say, "C'mon, man, just go with me for one beer. One beer. I've been working all night, I just want to go have one beer and unwind."

I'd say, "Dex, I gotta get up in the morning."

But he would always talk me into it. He was either the king of peer pressure or I was an easy mark. Probably both. Then we'd go out and next thing we'd close down some joint at two-thirty in the morning. Every time he'd laugh and say, "I can't believe you fell for the one-beer line again!" I think he set a record by getting me to go out eleven nights in a row.

I got him back, though.

Every guy has a dream girl, his own little fantasy. From the time he got his first erection, Dex's dream was his older sister's best friend. Unfortunately, she never paid much attention to Dex, and one day she got married and moved away. But while Dex and I shared the apartment, she came down to visit Dex's sister for the weekend. At the same time, Dex's childhood best friend, Gary, stayed with us.

One night, when Dex had to work the graveyard shift, Gary, Dex's sister, her friend, and I went out dancing and later ended up back at our place. Sometime in the middle of the night I got up and stumbled into the kitchen for a glass of water. Then a noise made me stop in my tracks. I snuck a peek into the living room and saw Gary and Dex's sister's married girlfriend going at it.

Since they didn't have any idea I was just around the corner, I managed to hide myself and watch. Gary did quite a number. I think there were bonus points being awarded left and right. I saw things that I had never imagined could happen with a coffee table and a sofa. This was rugged.

The next morning the girls left and Gary and I went to pick up Dex and have breakfast. Dex wanted to drive so I sat in the front and Gary in the back. Then Dex said, "So what'd you guys do last night?"

"We went out and had a few drinks," I said.

Dex just grunted.

"You know what might be interesting?" I continued. "Ask Gary what *he* did last night."

Gary punched me around the side of the seat. Dex just kept driving. I couldn't let it go. "Remember your dream girl, your one-and-only, your true love forever?"

Dex thought about it for a minute. "Yeah," he said. "She's visiting my sister."

"Well Gary did her on the coffee table last night."

"NOOOOOO!!!!" Dex swerved the car into a ditch.

"Sure," I continued. "When I looked in the living room, I thought I was watching a naked rodeo."

"NOOOO!!!!"

I know it might seem like I did a cruel thing, but I had to. Gary was *never* going to mention it, and I had Dex in such a vulnerable position that I felt obligated to destroy him. It was the guy thing to do. Besides, Gary had too much history with Dex to break his heart that way. Aren't men odd? You can ruin a man's dream, as long as you don't talk about it to his face.

Dex being Dex, he got over it.

While we're on the subject of women here's a classic story I've been dying to tell for a couple chapters already. Now that we're all grown-up, I think this is finally the place.

I was with another friend of mine, Wally Pace, at the Monday Night Football Game, watching the Falcons play the Rams at Fulton County Stadium. We were drinking boilermakers at the food concourse with some of my coworkers from Kroger. We quickly got as drunk as coots, sang beer songs, and leered at the local scenery. Then a woman in a green dress walked by. Wally said, "Hey! Do you believe in love at first sight?" She turned around and kind of laughed, and said, "I don't know." Wally stood up, wobbled over to her, and *kissed* her!

When they finally quit kissing he said, "Do you think it's love or lust."

She laughed again and said, "I don't know."

He said, "Do you want to go in the parking lot and find out?"

She said, "Why not?"

And they took off, leaving us to stand there with boilermakers in our hands, and our mouths hanging wide open. I know we all had the same thought: "This does not happen to anybody."

Halfway through the fourth quarter we saw little drunk Wally at the bottom of the steps, trying to find our seats. He ran up. Eddie Harlen said, "You didn't do it." Wally made Eddie smell the perfume on his shirt and elsewhere, and said, "*Tell me* I didn't do it!"

According to Pace the story went something like this: "We walked out of the stadium and I'm thinking, Where am I gonna do this? At first we thought about doing it on the grass outside but figured no, we'll surely get caught. Then I saw a bus driver sitting in his bus with the door open. She walked in front of me and over her head I waved at him, and signaled: 'Me, her, boom-boom-boom, your bus?' and the driver waved us over.

"But then I realize it might be too kinky and the guy would want to watch. So I ended up leaning her against the ladder of a Winnebago and we did it right there in the parking lot. When we finished, I said, 'What are you doing the rest of the night?' and she said, 'I really have to get back. I just went to buy my boyfriend a beer.' "

Ladies and gentleman: Casanova Wally Pace.

Single people have the best sex stories, even if they have girl-friends or boyfriends. I know one guy who told me he had scored just because he wanted to shoot some ducks. He had walked down to the lake with a young lady and when he suggested blasting a few water fowl she became horrified and said, "You're not going to shoot no ducks."

"Why not?"

"You're just not."

He thought about that for a minute. "Hmm. What's it worth to you for me not to shoot them?" he said to her.

Just like a guy, isn't it? She said, "I don't know." He said, "Let's go into my trailer and find out." Turns out it was worth quite a bit. Trailer park guys have all the luck. Later at dinner, he suddenly said, "Mmm. Ya know what? I feel like shooting some ducks."

"No, you aren't," his girlfriend said.

"Really, I want to."

"I said no."

They went outside to his car to argue. You know what? She somehow convinced him to be kind to animals after all.

Now you realize *why* we know that single people have the best sex stories. Because *they share them with everybody*. They slop on the intimate details. I didn't ask to hear this last story, but the guy couldn't help it. We all know these people. We see them in the break room at work. They always have a crowd gathered around. "So there I was, tied to the Black & Decker Workmate when she brings out the Shop Vac that cleans both wet and dry. Next night we did it with motor oil smeared all over our bodies. I also love it when she comes into the bedroom with a saddle and a set of jumper cables."

Married people just can't compete with this. What are we going to come back with? "You know, last night Marge vacuumed in her good robe. When she bent down to get underneath the sofa, I saw her butt. I started to get excited until I realized I could watch Hoss on *Bonanza* anytime!"

Married sex doesn't quite hold up, does it?

One problem with roommates is that they're always borrowing your stuff. Clothes, food, women. Dex used to borrow my car. His was a piece of crap. He called it Bob, for Beast of Burden. You could hear Bob coming eight blocks away, ten minutes before Dex got home. I had a Datsun 240Z. I'd wake up and there'd be a note that read, "Jeff. Took the car. If the police call, just report it stolen." I would never know how long he'd had it.

One night Dex loaned Bob to some friends and they called us at two in the morning and said, "Dex, your car has broken down in the middle of the road and we can't move it. What should we do?" We were too wasted to move. I took the phone away from him and said, "You do not understand: We cannot leave the house." They said, "Well, we're just going to leave the car in the middle of the road."

"Do what you have to do," I said. "If we get in my car to come over there, we will never get out of jail again."

We got Bob back the next day, but he wasn't long for the road. One night Bob broke down again on the soft shoulder. Dex said it needed water. I scampered down the hillside with empty beer bottles and found water in a ditch, in the dark. We kept filling up the beer bottles and pouring them into Bob. After about fifteen trips we decided to crank the engine. Bob went "pffflt" and died. About that time someone stopped by with a flashlight and shined it in Bob's radiator and we discovered it was full of tadpoles. We left Bob there and never went back to get him.

RIP, Bob.

One day, just like Bob's demise, the roommate experience is over. You move on. Maybe it's to a place of your own, or your own room back at the folks', or if you're lucky, you meet the significant other of your dreams. That's what happened to me. I met Gregg.

I was wild in my single days, but I think that's okay. I can't apologize for trying to milk everything there is out of life. I had to go through, not around, the experience of trying it all. But one day I realized that my wallet and my back and my heart couldn't take it anymore. I couldn't continue to do all the stuff my parents told me never to do—because it was fun—and remain employed and a viable member of society.

I didn't actually think that clearly at the time. I worked pretty much on pure instinct. Let's just say I knew that if I didn't sow the wild oats and flush the tadpoles out of my system, then I might one day break down and be left on the roadside after giving in to the temptation to try that stuff under inappropriate circumstances, like when I was married with children.

I knew it was time to grow up.

From This Day Forth...

The whole time I worked in Sarasota I nagged IBM to transfer me back to Atlanta. I missed my family, I missed the great state of Georgia, and for some reason I couldn't get a date if my life depended on it. They finally broke down and sent me home in April 1984. The following month my buddies threw me a "Welcome Home" party. I spent much of the evening on the balcony, drinking beer, telling stories, and making people laugh. Finally, Rob Burkett, who also worked at IBM, said,

"Have you ever thought about going onstage at the comedy club? We go down there all the time."

I said, "No, I've never even *been* in a comedy club."

"Well, go with me next week and watch."

The next Tuesday I sat through the agony and the ecstasy of amateur night. Afterward I said, "Okay, I'll try that." Compared to shooting doves at the airport and jumping off a moving truck onto a hay bale at forty miles an hour, five minutes on a stage seemed unlikely to get me into much trouble or cause great pain.

At home I wrote some material about my family. One bit was about Big Jim's toenails, and how toenails change as you age. Another joke was: "When people celebrate a football win they tear down the goalposts and carry them over their heads. Life doesn't really work like that, does it. When you sleep with someone for the first time, do you tear off the headboard and run around the apartment complex? I have, however, spiked a couple of pair of panties."

Horrible stuff, but I did it for Rob and my brother. They laughed loudly enough that I decided to take the next step. I'd risk my reputation as a funny guy in the IBM break room and repeat my routine in front of total strangers who didn't give a damn about me because all they wanted was more to drink and for the headliner to come out and make them laugh. There was only one problem. When we called the Punchline to get a spot on amateur night they told us it was temporarily canceled for the summer because for the next twelve weeks the club was hosting the prelims for the Great Southeastern Laugh Off.

"Wait a few months," they suggested. However, we were extremely fired up, so Rob got everybody he worked with to call the Punchline and ask, "Is Jeff Foxworthy going to be on next Tuesday?"

"I don't know, why?"

"If so we'd like to bring forty people." It was a total bluff. You'd think comedy clubs would have caught on by now. But by the time they got the fiftieth phone call the club owners had probably decided that they couldn't take the chance that it was a hoax; they had to think instead about paid admissions and big liquor sales. So the people at the Punchline said, "Yeah, he's gonna be on." No one went down except Rob and me, but I did get my spot—on last—in a contest that was really only for working comedians.

That night was the only time in my career I've needed a drink to perform. Four Seven & Seven's did the trick. I was still so nervous I could not look at anybody, so I stared at the floor instead. My first words before paying customers were: "I am a virgin comedian. This is my first time."

I won my night, eventually made it to the semifinals, and came in fifth overall. They only took four finalists and I'd missed it by half a point. My mistake? My set went too long.

That first time I was thrilled because I had actually gotten laughs. Without laughs there never would have been a second time, I promise you. However, figuring that my first five minutes had worked, I brimmed with confidence and wrote a new five minutes. Then I went on at another local club, Jerry Farber's. Rob went with me and this time brought people. I went totally down the toilet.

Even so, I knew I had found my calling.

A new career would have been enough, but the night was still young. I didn't know it, but my future wife was in the audience that first night at the Punchline. We didn't know each other. I don't remember this, but she later told me she came up and said "Congratulations." Gregg thought the "virgin" routine was just part of my act and that I was a working comic from Florida. When she got to know me better, she also told me she thought I was a snob because all I did that night was say to her, "Oh, thanks," and turn away. The truth is that I was a nervous wreck. If I'd known better

I would have paid more attention at the time. Anyone who reads women's magazines like I do (a man's got to take something up in the tree to pass the time) will know that they're full of articles insisting that what women want first and foremost in a man is a sense of humor. Take some advice from a guy who's never had any trouble making people laugh: This can't be true. Every woman in the world could say "sense of humor" until the cows come home, but you never see women throwing their panties onstage at a comedy club. Except in those rare circumstances, like when you have a top-ten-rated TV show or you're the last man on the planet, comics don't have groupies.

Fortunately, Gregg also told a friend she thought I was cute. Unfortunately, I only learned this after three years of marriage, during a fight about whose family was crazier, when she took it back.

We met again a few months later when the friend who'd taken her to the club the first time decided to go onstage on amateur night at the Punchline herself, and she talked Gregg into being her audience. At first Gregg said, "I don't know if I want to go," but her friend said, "Well, Jeff Foxworthy's going to be there." (Said it provocatively, you understand.) So Gregg said, "Okay, I'll go." God bless her for being willing to give me another chance.

After the show we were formally introduced.

I remember trying to be cool because in the intervening months I had gained a little stature as one of the better amateur comics in Atlanta. (I was definitely funnier than the other two.) I recall exactly what she was wearing: tan pants and a little zigzag sweater over a white shirt. The sweater had no sleeves. I'd like to credit my romantic personality for remembering her outfit, but honestly, it's because I walked up and immediately spilled my drink down the front of her pants and sweater. After fumbling the kick off, so to speak, I was ready to forfeit the game.

"Well, I guess this means you'll never go out with me," I said.

She said, "You haven't even asked."

Time to throw the long bomb.

"Okay, will you go out with me?"

"Yeah."

Touchdown!

Boy, was I smiling on the outside. Inside I knew I was a dog. Not two days earlier I had returned from a weekend with a woman at a cabin in the South Carolina mountains. But once I met Gregg I forgot all about anyone else. I disappeared on this woman and never called her back. I imagine, as just retribution, that she's never written me a letter saying she's my biggest fan. She probably thinks I'm the scum of the earth.

Gregg and I spent the rest of the evening standing at the bar, talking. I discovered that Gregg was an actress who had just played the lead in a movie called *Ocean Drive Weekend*. She also did local commercials. I thought she was big-time show business, which didn't make her less interesting at all. However, it's good that besides wanting to hitch my wagon to a star, Gregg had other great qualities. I've always liked brunettes. I've always liked small women. I like them with spit and fire. She had all three.

Finally the lights came up and it was time for everyone to go home. Gregg and I had already planned to go out later that week, but as I said good-bye, I did something that I'd never done before without at least a date under my belt. I kissed her goodnight. This was not a little peck. I kissed her very well, which, in my book, involves cutting and shampooing my mustache, exercising my lips for ten to twenty seconds to warm up, and, if I'm in a really sexy mood, applying a little lip gloss and peach slicker.

Gregg later told me she'd never kissed a guy so soon before, either. I said that was nice, and that I'd *never* kissed a guy *at all*, even if I'd known him for years, and I hoped it wouldn't jeopardize our getting to know each other better. Now that I think about it, our first kiss was like that moment in *Annie Hall* when Woody Allen smooches Diane Keaton to "get it out of the way" before they get all tense about it at the end of their date. I'm no short, neurotic, brilliantly funny, New York comedian who ponders the ineffability of love and death and questions the nature of existence, but otherwise I like to think that I'm a lot like Mr. Allen.

"If you think challah is what you do when a tractor runs over your foot . . . you might be a Redneck."

As I was saying, I'm surprised that Gregg and I kissed. Watching a couple make out in public is not a pretty sight. I always think, "Oh my. Geez. I'm trying to keep some nachos down. Would you guys knock it off?" Stranger still, we'd both recently ended unsatisfying relationships and didn't want to get involved so soon again.

That was a Tuesday.

"Don't want to rush into anything," we both said.

The Saturday we went out Gregg had, coincidentally, just moved in with one of her best girlfriends, in Marietta, Georgia. I drove down to pick her up. While I waited in the living room for Gregg to get ready, her roommate said, "You're gonna be smitten." She didn't even know me, but she seemed sure that it would happen.

I took Gregg to a party. Sixty people were crammed into a little house. We walked in, grabbed two beers, and went directly to a bench on the back porch where, beyond the loud music, we sat and talked for hours. We were oblivious to everyone and everything, although we did stop talking for a moment to watch a woman dancing by herself in the corner.

"Hey, it's only 8:30 and Peggy's dancing by herself," I said. "That shirt's coming off tonight, I guarantee it."

Gregg looked at me like I was some kind of cretin.

"Just part of the act. Just the act, I promise."

Then we got lost in each other.

Three hours later we realized it was three hours later. I know this sounds stupid, but honestly, all I remember is that at some point early in the conversation I looked at Gregg and thought,

"I'm gonna marry this girl." She must have been thinking about forever, too, because that's when she said, "Honey, would you mind getting me another beer?"

It was all I could do to not blurt out, "Will you marry me?" right there.

On the way back to Gregg's I decided that I would be a perfect gentleman at the door because I didn't want to screw up my long-term possibilities. No way did I want her thinking, "Oh gee, we get to the door and he starts pawing me like a cougar." I wasn't going to do any leaning in on the leg. None of the poodle-on-the-living-room-floor stuff.

I hope I'm not confusing you with these Redneck mating terms. The first means that when you're kissing a woman, you lean in and make them aware of your package.

"What the hell is that?"

"Sorry. I've got a severe thigh cramp."

I don't know what the second term means, but it sounded intriguing. There are other moves. The accidental forearm across the breast is always a good one. Hand sliding down to the rear end is another.

"Oh, gosh, I didn't realize my hand was on your butt."

"Well get it off or you'll really have a severe thigh cramp."

The most serious move is kidnapping.

So far I haven't had to resort to that.

I kissed Gregg goodnight, then I backed away and said, "I'll call you." To my surprise, Gregg just grinned and said, "Get in the house."

"Alll-riiight, okay, going in the house now."

I believe she might have put the chain on the door. Good sign and exactly what I wanted, not that I had anything to do with it. Although my fortunes had brightened I certainly wasn't going to initiate anything, even if I had made it over the threshold. You've got to go through the little ritual. You can't just walk in the door and go straight to the bedroom and say, "Where do I hang my pants?"

I'm glad we stayed in the living room to talk. One of the first things Gregg told me was, "You've got to get out of your job at IBM. You've got too much stuff trying to come out of you."

I said, "If you only knew . . ." I was impressed that she had encouraged my need to entertain and be funny, on the first date. This made me even more crazy about her.

Then she did something funny. She walked toward the bedroom and said, "Enough chat. Come in here, I want to show you something."

Clown paintings. She had clown paintings!

I wish I could say that before I knew it I heard birds chirping and it was the next morning. But at the time I lived in my mother's basement. So I had to get up before our passion cooled and call Carole. How impressive is that? I said, "You know, Mom, it's really late. I'm across town. I think I'm just going to stay at Rob's house tonight." It was pretty embarrassing. I'd met the true love of my life and I had to say, "I need to call my mother." Fortunately, Gregg didn't react badly at all. She laughed. She'd just moved out of her dad's house. She knew exactly what I was going through.

The next morning I had to face Gregg's roommate. I had that good-morning hair and the previous night's disco clothes. I said, "Hi, how are you? You guys have any orange juice?" One look at her face and I knew what she was thinking, "What kind of slut have I moved in with? She's here for eight hours and . . ."

"By the way," I said. "You were right. I'm smut."

"I told you so," she said.

After that night Mr. Slow-and-Easy became like a tick. You could have burned my butt with three thousand hot match heads, and I still wouldn't have let go. We were inseparable. We went out every night. Saturday, Sunday, Monday, Tuesday, and Wednesday. On Thursday morning we finally decided, "Whoa, better slow down. Remember, neither of us wants to get involved. This is going really fast. Thursday night we will not see each other." That lasted until about nine that night, when I called Gregg and we talked for forty minutes on the phone. I said, "Let's meet for a drink somewhere," and we did. After that we were more or less living together. My routine became: go to work, get off, meet Gregg.

I had to keep telling my mom that I was staying at Rob Burkett's. I was an adult and could do what I wanted, but moms are sensitive that way. No one wants their kid to walk around with a large "Living in Sin" sign stamped on their forehead. Besides, my mom is a religious woman. It's a wonder she didn't get suspicious of me and Rob, since Carole thought Rob was really cute. I *guess* that's what she meant when she said, "Rob Burkett would be handsome in a barrel." Come to think of it, she probably could have handled the news that Rob and I were in love more easily.

Eventually, I told my mom I was moving out of the basement and in with Big Jim across town. I didn't go there much except to grab some clothes.

Once again, Gregg urged me to quit my job at IBM and try comedy full-time, and I finally took her advice. When I walked out the door at Big Blue on December 31, 1984, I had eleven minutes of material. I banked my career on that. Nobody knew me. Most of the time they didn't care. I was just a distraction while people got drinks and chatted before the headliner came on. Even so, I spent my entire day getting ready to work fifteen minutes a night.

About five weeks into this new arrangement Gregg realized I wasn't making any money. So she did the only thing she could do, besides dump me at the roadside like Bob the car. She quit acting and doing commercials and took a full-time job to support my dream. What can I say? All I could do was wonder what I'd done to deserve this woman. I still think that. Within twenty minutes on a night in June 1984, I'd not only discovered what I wanted to do with the rest of my life, but I'd also met the woman with whom I wanted to spend it. That's even better than bagging a deer, catching the biggest lake bass, and sleeping with every woman De-Wayne Twilley has known—all at once. That's really saying something.

When a man is with the right woman, one day he must actually declare his love. Saying, "I really like you," "I'm crazy for you," or "You're more fun than the Home Ec. teacher" just won't cut it anymore. I'd bit my lip bloody for weeks, trying not to tell Gregg that I'd loved her from the first date. Finally, I couldn't contain myself. We were standing in a restaurant parking lot, three weeks after our first night together, and I said, "I've got to tell you something."

She said, "Don't."

I said, "No, I've got to."

"Don't."

"No, I've got to tell you this."

"*Please* don't."

"I love you."

"Oh my God."

The worst part is that she didn't say it back. When you say you love a woman and she doesn't respond in kind, certain things go through your head like, "She's going to change her phone number in the morning." Suddenly I felt like a candidate for one of those talk shows where you have the tearful reunion five years later.

HOST: *Remember you were going out. You had a great time. He said "I love you." You disappeared and moved to Nevada. Well, now he's rich, he's famous, and he's still single. Here he is again!*

ME: *(looking very sharp, but wiping a small tear from my eye)* Hi.

GREGG: *(impressed) I do love him. I just forgot to say it. He's rich? Yeah, I love him!*

That's her joke now: She married me for my money.

If you're looking for advice about saying "I love you" first or holding out, don't look here. Once you're in love, you just become stupid. Part of you thinks, "Don't say this yet. She hasn't given any indication that she's gonna say it back. Bide your time. It's going well. Ride it out." But that "in-love" part of your brain goes, "It's okay, just say it. Just damn well say it! Shout it from the rooftops!" That part always overrides everything else. I've only said it to a few women and I've always meant it, except for a couple of times when the woman in question was sitting on top of me. Naked.

Here we were falling for each other and it felt as glorious as screaming "Free Bird" at a Lynyrd Skynyrd concert. Although Gregg didn't say she loved me, I wasn't afraid that she'd suddenly leave me. I knew that because the first night she'd told me that she had promised herself never to get involved with another man unless he was smart, funny, and sexy. She *had* to have all three. Being an insecure, amateur-night comic, I waited until morning and asked: "All right, so how many out of the three do I get?" I don't have to tell you the answer, do I?

Maybe I do, but I won't. I was raised right.

Eventually, Gregg uttered the magic words. "Honey, would you mind picking up some barbeque on the way home?" She also confessed to being in love with me. Before long we began to talk about marriage. Well, I talked about it. We'd moved in together, I wanted to get married. She didn't. I hounded her for a little while, then decided to let it go. Suddenly she "kind of" wanted to get married. I pouted and said, "No. You broke my heart. You didn't want to get married when I wanted to get married, so now I don't want to get married." So we stopped talking about it altogether, but only for a while.

The summer after I met Gregg I again entered the Great Southeastern Laugh Off at the Punchline, and this time won it all. Part of the prize was $500 and a trip to New York to play at Catch-a-Rising-Star in Manhattan. Gregg and I went up together. I had no money. She had a credit card. We stayed at a place on 49th and Broadway. Great neighborhood. Looking out our bedroom window we could see a huge movie theater marquee across the street. I'll always remember what was playing: *Horny Sluts*.

Give my regards to Broadway.

Since we were in town and flush, we decided to get married. We'd talked about it enough and New York seemed like a cool place. No family or friends, no hassles. I called a comedian friend of mine, Rob Bartlett, who is a very funny guy and, at the time, was the *only* guy I knew in New York. I said, "We've decided to get married. I need a best man." We went to City Hall to get a marriage license. Then we started looking for a justice of the peace. We couldn't find one in the phone book, so I called churches. Finally one minister said he'd marry us and only charge $300.

"I don't have $300," I said. "Why is it so much?"

"Well, it's $200 for the chapel and $100 for me."

"Look, we don't need the chapel," I said. "We can do this in your office. Do it in the hall. Even out back."

"You know what?" he said. "I'm right across the street from the garden at Central Park. If you want, I'll walk across the street and do it for $100."

I said, "You've got a deal. Thursday at noon."

When the time came I wore a $35 suit. It had no lining. I think
it was part of the prize for winning the Laugh Off. I've still got it
for special occasions. Rob Bartlett showed up with his wife, who
was about eight months pregnant, and a twenty-pound bag of rice
he'd bought on the way. Then Reverend Leonard arrived.

We had our vows ready.

> ME: *Hey, you know, man, I'm gonna try an stop foolin'
> around with other wimmens now and everything. You know I
> love you.*
>
> SHE: *What with the baby comin' and everything, I figured
> we might as well get married.*
>
> ME: *She likes to party.*
>
> SHE: *And so does he.*
>
> ME: *(To her dad) It's okay, man, put that shotgun down.*
> *I'm pledgin everlastin' luuuvvv.*

Bet you believed it for just a second.

It was a fine day for a wedding. Just the four of us; oh, and the
guy sweeping the park, around the fountain in the garden. We had
to plead with him to move out of the way so we could get married.
He stood to the side while the Reverend recited the standard ceremony. Afterwards the sweeper said, "Please, please don't throw
that rice or I'll have to clean up again."

"But we've got to throw the rice," I said.

Bartlett gave him twenty bucks and he was happy. He's also in
our four wedding pictures. That was part of the deal. There we are:
me, Gregg, the Bartletts, Reverend Leonard, and Andre the park
sweeper, who also somehow managed to get his arm around my
new wife.

By the way, I hear you're not supposed to throw rice anymore
at weddings. Bird seed is preferred. Apparently the birds eat the
rice, then when they drink water the rice puffs up, and the birds
explode. Really. Forget the wedding. I'd pay $100 to see that.

Afterward we took the Bartletts to the Tavern on the Green for
lunch. Then Gregg tried to inject a little culture into my life and

we went to see two plays. Between the first and the second we called our respective families from a phone booth to give them the big news.

It's better that way, believe me.

No matter what your love life is like before marriage, the vows change everything. This is probably not news to anyone except hermit crabs and certain movie stars who keep marrying and hoping for something to change. (Remember, insanity is doing the same thing over and over while expecting a different result.) But considering all the advice books sold on how to find a mate, please your mate, talk to your mate (and, for beginners, how to tell the difference between potential mates and common barnyard animals), it's not like everyone's doing such a great job here. We seem to need all the help we can get. So please, benefit from my experience, or my complete naivete. Whichever works in a pinch.

FRIENDS

Even before you're hitched, your friends put out an all-points bulletin that you're missing in action. At first they wait to see if you're just having another of your renowned three-week relationships: court them, catch them, cash them in. But if it continues longer, then they can't avoid the Truth: you're no longer available to trade babe stories, pull all-nighters, and bar hop—unless you can do it in the living room, with the wife's permission, after she falls asleep. Even so, this doesn't help much because your friends will still resent your woman for taking you away from them. And she will be uptight because when you entertain the old gang, she has to listen to them tell stories about the crazy things you did when you were single.

Later, when you're lying in bed hoping to get lucky, she'll say, "Tell me you did not moon a bus full of nuns."

"I didn't know they were nuns."

"How could you not know?"

"I wasn't *looking* at them."

"It was still your ass on the window. You ought to be ashamed of yourself. Goodnight."

Fortunately, you don't have to shoulder all the blame. Whimper enough and your wife will turn back in your direction and say, "I know you couldn't have done it all by yourself, honey. It's those no-account friends. I love yew."

Such is the power of rationalization and, if you're really in the doghouse, tears.

The smart man reveals as little as possible about his past activities and convinces his friends to do likewise if they want to have any hope of seeing him again in their lifetimes. You can tell some cute little stories, but the trip to Mexico to see Pepe the Wonder Donkey is probably one to keep close to the vest.

Even more important, never talk about old girlfriends. I'm always stunned and amazed when I meet couples who tell each other in graphic detail everything that they've done sexually with other people before they met. I hear that sometimes this can be a stimulating marital aid, but even so, Gregg and I made a pact immediately: We didn't want to know any intimate details of previous relationships. I don't want to hear about it. My imagination's too vivid.

So as far as I know, neither Gregg nor I have been with anyone before being with each other.

INTIMATE RELATIONS

Marriage alters both the quantity and quality of your intimate relations. Anyone who says it doesn't is either single or lying. With married sex you never have to worry about dislocating your shoulder. With single sex, you always do it like there's a crowd watching and someone's keeping score. Initially, married sex is really not *that* much different from single sex, but the longer you do it the tougher it is to find ways keep it interesting. Finally, you're just trying to find ways to stay awake. (I say that in jest, honey, because I want to *continue* to have sex.)

A big difference between married and single sex is that the former now seems to take place much more within the home, and specifically the bedroom. I don't know what women do, but when guys get together they will eventually talk about the weirdest places they've gotten lucky. That's always a fascinating conversation. Not always believable, but still compelling.

I know one guy who was quite proud of doing it on top of an off-balanced Maytag washing machine in the middle of spin cycle. Apparently that was the key: in the middle of spin cycle. Seems you get some type of vibrations there that you can't get anywhere else on the planet.

Another guy once told me he did it in a deer stand twenty-five feet off the ground.

"Didn't see any deer, didn't give a damn."

"What about the silence is golden hunting rule?"

"Lifted it."

What's truly amazing is that he was a sane, rational person who had a good job, made his mortgage payments, and knew exactly what to do if a deer wandered past while he was mating in a tree.

"Stop, reach for the shotgun, and fire. You should always keep the gun nearby, with one in the chamber. Deer don't come along that often. But if you've got a romantic bone in your body, you finish the act before you clean the deer."

My point is that when you're married you *have* to keep things interesting. I've sometimes thought, "Why didn't we try this five years ago?" But then I guess it just never occurred to me to bring a spatula to bed.

SIGNS ALONG THE WAY

To have any chance of sex materializing, all the proper signs and signals must happen. When you're single, a stop sign will suffice.

If it's not a busy intersection, what the hey? When you're married, other important considerations arise:

1. Does she have to get up early for work?

2. Is any family member in the midst of a crisis, and could he or she call and force you to discuss it at an inconvenient time?

3. Are the dishes washed? Women can't do it with dirty dishes in the sink. I don't know why, but the smell of rotting food does not stimulate the sex glands. My advice: Learn to wash dishes. It's mindless, relaxing, they've got soap that won't chaff your hands, and if you don't tell on me I won't tell on you.

4. Body temperature is important. If it's too hot or too cold, you ain't doing it, buddy.

"You want to do it?"

"Oh, God, it's so hot, I couldn't possibly do it."

"You want to do it?"

"Oh, God, it's too cold." The trick is to lie and say, "Okay, we'll stay under the covers." After you get started you can whip them off.

"You oughta be warm by now! Yee-hah!"

5. Physical problems. Has the missus had any significant aches or pains in the last thirty minutes? If she's free and clear, make your move. The longer you wait the higher the odds against you. This is purely a gender thing. Guys could cut their knee off with a chain saw and before they go to the hospital if the wife said, "You want to do it?" they'd say, "Okay, we'll put a towel around it. Could somebody hold the ambulance?"

6. What she's wearing. Check what the little woman's wearing to bed. If it's something she can rake leaves in, you're out of luck. Or in for the kinkiest night of your life.

Oh, by the way, no shirt, no shoes, no problem.

If you've made it this far, sorry—there's still a way to go. Once you've mastered these basic issues, you simply get to move on to more complicated ones.

7. Cycles. According to medical science, guys get interested in sex roughly every ninety minutes. And we talk about it for the other eighty-seven. This even happens when we're asleep. Sometimes you wake up right in the middle of a dream about you and the latest *Playboy* Playmate and you want to do it. Unfortunately, not many women want their men rousing them from REM sleep expecting something he didn't make reservations for two days in advance. I don't understand that. I'd even accept, "Okay, but try not to wake me."

8. Sex and food. The adage that the way to a man's heart is through his stomach is generally true. If my wife wants her way with me she fixes me something I like to eat. But you've got to be careful not to overeat. Sex is not a good idea *after* eating. There's nothing worse than sleeping on a full stomach, especially hers. Big Jim told me that nothing kills passion quicker than a distended belly. Big Jim says you can do it if you've had too much to drink, you can do it you've had too little sleep. But you cannot do it on a full stomach, unless it's yours and then you want to be on top.

9. What's on TV? Be careful what you watch on TV as your foreplay. The story about the kid whose parents died and left him in an alley where he raised himself and survived by eating from a dumpster is not going to help. It can't be anything tearful. Stay away from *20/20* and *Nightline* and any infomercial featuring exercise equipment, chatty Aussies, or motivational demigods. You don't want your woman motivated to exercise and run away with Mel Gibson.

10. Watch the clock. Depending on how much sleep your partner has had during the week, you could still get the arched eyebrow at 12:10. Or it could already be too late at 9:40.

"I thought we were going to do it tonight."

"It's too late."

"It's 9:40! For God's sakes, *ER's* not on yet! We could do it and *still* watch *ER.*"

11. Real foreplay. The most important thing to remember about sex after marriage is that you have to warm up your woman. (The second most important thing is afterplay. Any intelligent man knows it greases the way for the next time.) With the spontaneity of single life gone, women became hard machines to start. Everybody's had a lawn mower they couldn't kick over. You add gas, check the oil, and pull the choke, and still nothing. It *should* run better. Maybe it would if you used it more than twice a month when the grass grows, and let it idle once a week in the winter. If *men* were lawnmowers they might *look* like crap but they'd start up on the first pull and run until the last drop of gas got sucked into the carburetor.

Tell you a little secret. Men always say they long for a woman who starts up like a man, but I think most of us would get bored if it was too easy. We might kick and scream and insist we wouldn't, but it's true. A good analogy is the thrill of fishing. If every time you threw in your line you instantly caught a fish and pulled it out, fishing wouldn't be very much fun, would it? You've got to put on the right bait, deliver the line smoothly, retrieve it with finesse. Then when you get one, you're proud. "Man, I must be pretty cool. I got a fish."

Now, coincidentally, you know why women *aren't* big fisherman. They toss out their line and men *always* take the bait. Doesn't matter what she looks like, a woman can always get some guy interested. (Yes, I know. A woman's reason for fishing is not the same as a man's. Women actually have to *like* the fish.) That, my friends, is why *women make a game out of sex*. They know they *can* get it anytime. They've *always* known it. It's in some book they all get when they're born, I'm sure.

Another reason men don't really want a woman who is overly eager is that we're so insecure that we're always thinking, "If I can start her up so quick then what is she doing while I'm at work?'' Men like to think they're the only ones with the keys to the machine. Men have good reason to be insecure. Haven't you woken up in the morning and done it before either of you have brushed your teeth? Then you walk into the bathroom, look in the mirror, and think your hair looks like frame 237 of the Zapruder film. Plus, you're breath is horrible, you've got gunk in the corner of your eye, and a little trace of drool down your chin. You think, ''My God, if my woman would do it with *this*, she will do it with anybody.''

And if she wanted to, you can't stop her. Women have all the power. Men have none. They're like Caesar's wife at the gladiator show in the Coliseum. Do one thing wrong and it's thumbs-down.

12. Be romantic. The old cliché is that women give sex to get love and men give love to get sex. So what else is new? Men are not, by nature, romantic creatures. But I think we discovered early on in the game that if you don't learn how to be romantic, you're not going to win very often. So we shamble and ask, ''What is romance?'' Too bad we don't like the answers: ''Comb my hair nice? Put down the remote control? What if I spray-paint your name on the side of the house? I don't give a damn about the neighbors. I want to tell the whole world how I feel about you.''

If only we could. In the end we're like circus bears. We need to be trained to do what we must to get the reward at the end of the act.

You know what? We gladly do it.

Since the night I first told Gregg I loved her, I've not gone a single day without saying it, and meaning it. Each day I also remind her that she's the prettiest girl in the whole world. One more thing: Because ours is the greatest love story known to man, in the twelve years since we met I have never, ever farted in front of my wife. Take me on a camping trip and I can clear out a pup tent pretty quick. But never in front of Gregg.

Maybe I'm not such a Redneck after all.

...Till Death Do Us Part

You know you're married when you're lying in bed with somebody and you suddenly think, "Uh oh, I've got to go home, my wife's waiting on me."

Never happened to me, of course.

I walked into my marriage with my eyes open and have never regretted it. Never fooled around and never wanted to. But once or twice, I've had those moments where I suddenly realized I was married—as if I could ever forget—and wondered how I'd gotten there. The first time that happened, I made an important discovery that you can only make *after* you're married: The person you were dating who said "I wouldn't change anything about you" was *lying*.

It's not just a female trait.

But it's *mostly* a female trait.

No wonder marriage is a big decision: It's the choice between the freedom to live as you please or with someone else's relentless analysis of your shortcomings.

Have you ever heard women in the supermarket checkout line talk about what their men were like before they met them? It's almost as if they'd captured and tamed wild animals.

"First time I saw Tom, he was naked on the side of the road, eating roots and kudzu with his bare hands. I took him home, taught him how to wear a shirt and eat with a spoon, and later we got him a job. Still eats roots. If you don't watch him like a hawk, he'll pull his clothes off and go out in the backyard and start digging around the trees."

Among women, the things they've gotten their husbands to do are a badge of honor. "Since he met me, Narvel takes a shower every Saturday, whether he needs it or not." This is usually the prelude to the conversation about the stuff their husbands *still* won't do. "Then I said, 'How about if we get naked in the satellite dish?' But I don't think he heard me over the football scores."

Women are shameless. Sometimes just for fun, and right out in public, they'll compete with other women they don't even know, over whose husband most embraced and abused the notion of bachelor living.

"Before we got married, Ed's refrigerator had a potato inside that was *alive*. I had to kill it."

"Oh yeah? I donated the mold on Randy's shower curtain to the CDC. They took one look at it under a microscope and found a cure for jock itch."

"Earl slept with the light on."

"What's so bad about that?"

"Every morning he couldn't figure out why the car wouldn't start."

When I see this happen, I have to laugh softly to myself. Any man would because we're all thinking the same thing: "Yeah? So what? *You slept with me.* What does that say about you?"

Most women are obsessed with clothes. I don't mean their clothes. (This book would be twice as long if I wrote about that subject.) When a woman wants to change a man, she often begins with his wardrobe. The whole time you're dating she never says anything when you wear hip waders to the covered dish Christmas dinner. She thinks it's cute. But women are sneaky. Once you're sharing a bedroom and closet, she will get rid of your clothes when you're not looking. All of a sudden there's so many bags of stuff marked "charity" that the Salvation Army pulls up in an eighteen-wheeler. I once came home from the road and discovered that Gregg had done me "a favor" and "cleaned out" my closet. I immediately ripped through the boxes she'd piled in the hall.

"You can't get rid of this shirt!" I said.

"But it's out of style."

"Out of style? Are you kidding me? When I watched *Bewitched* last night Darren had on one just like it. That's not out of style!"

Men aren't stupid. We know it's out of style. We're just waiting for it to come back.

What's even worse is that if your wife spends any time going through your things, your clothes start to smell like her perfume. Then you can't wear anything because your friends will give you a hard time.

"You smell nice, Jeff. New fabric softener? Haw, haw."

This is one reason why it's always a good idea to keep your hunting clothes in the garage, ready for an emergency.

Heaven forbid that I would ever go into Gregg's closet and do *her* a favor. I wouldn't dare think about it because (a) I'm too lazy to do it, and (b) I just wouldn't dare.

I might *fool around* in her closet, though. I've cleaned out her underwear drawer occasionally and put everything back where I found it. (Never a problem. As you know, I graduated from Big Jim's College of Leaving It Like You Found It.) I also check to see what new accessories she's bought. I keep hoping to find something frilly and exciting, but it pretty much comes down to belts and shoes. I've got three belts and three pairs of shoes. She's got 700 belts. I'm still counting the shoes.

Women have too much choice. Any time we dress to go out with friends she says, "I can't wear that."

"Why not?"

"I wore it six months ago. The last time we saw these people."

"So? How are they going to know?" I can't tell you what *I* wore yesterday."

When women go out, they come home and talk about what other women wore. "Did you see the Jaclyn Smith skirt Darlene had on? I know I saw it last week on the K Mart closeout table." Never do you see two guys leaving the bowling alley at the end of the evening going, "Did you see the shirt Fred was wearing? Oh my God. And those pants, they had to be from last year. Come on Fred, show some fashion sense, for God's sake."

Women also try to get you to cut your hair a different way, and to care for it with their girly conditioners. Why they think it's a waste of perfectly good automotive products to use transmission fluid to keep a pompadour set is beyond me. Besides, it gives your hair an Elvis-like sheen.

Guys don't want to change a lot about women. Guys just like consistency. They want more food, less nagging, and more sex. As regularly as possible. Otherwise, men are pretty flexible. If a woman suddenly stopped her share of the housekeeping duties and the dishes piled up in the sink, a guy would think, "Oh, we've chosen a new lifestyle. Okay, I can do this. I've done this before when I lived with Boomer.''

One thing we don't want is a lot of questions. For instance, ''What are you thinking?'' When two guys ride together in a truck, never does one turn to the other and go, ''Chuck, whatcha thinking?'' Ask a woman what she's thinking and it's either about your shortcomings or about food. You've got to feed them regularly to keep them out of a bad mood because that's when they start thinking about what's wrong with you. (Everything in a woman's universe is connected, Buddha buddy.) I don't know how often my wife and I have been on the road together and she's said, ''If I don't eat soon, I'm going to get a headache.'' I've ridden a billion miles with guys and I have never heard a man say, ''God, if I don't eat soon, I'm gonna be hell to live with. Scratch the hell out of the dashboard, I'll tell you that. I don't want to get pissy, but I need fries.''

I don't know what women want. We married them, but that doesn't seem to be enough. I think they'd rather have great-looking shoes that are comfortable. Eyeliner that doesn't run. And jewelry. I hear you can never go wrong at the jewelry well.

My wife doesn't deny it, but I get the feeling that even if she had all that it still wouldn't be sufficient.

''I just want you to show me some attention,'' she always says.

''Sure thing, sugar dumpling,'' I always answer. ''At halftime.''

One satisfying aspect of marriage is attending your friends' weddings and trying not to fall on the floor laughing because they have no idea what married life will be like. Just because they'd lived together since they were brother and sister doesn't mean a thing. You'll also laugh at yourselves because you know that no matter how hard you try, there's no way to explain it to them.

Even so, weddings typically offer the best entertainment value for your community property dollar. I remember when my friend

Jimmy got married. I was one of six groomsmen. We decided right before we arrived at the church that we were going to convince Jimmy that he had a cliff-hanger; in other words, something in his nose. Jimmy came out and stood near the altar. As each of us walked down the aisle to join him, we'd point discreetly to our noses. Jimmy spent his entire wedding picking at his nose. He would look over at us like, "Did I get it?" We'd look back and silently mouth, "Nah, you didn't get it." The whole thing is on video. I can get you a copy.

Once or twice I've wondered what it would be like to be a woman. I think I'd probably get kicked out of public places for playing with my breasts a lot. "Ma'am, you're going to have to stop fondling yourself in front of the other diners."

Seriously, I would love to sit around with women and talk to them *as* a woman and find out what they really want from men. Guys *are* totally clueless. But even if I discovered the secret, changed back to a man, and told my friends, they probably wouldn't believe me.

"Nah, Jeff. It couldn't be *that*. You musta heard it wrong."

Things change slowly, as Don Henley once sang on the Eagles' *Long Run* album, "if they ever change at all." So it is with couples. It's only when spouses accept that they can't really change each other that the mature marriage becomes possible. With the pressure gone to be someone else, each of you gets to relax and be who you are. There are risks, however. The shock of realizing who your husband or wife *really is* could make you feel as if you just fell into a mountain brook in the middle of winter. You'll instantly go numb and just want to get out as soon as possible. Or with nothing left to nag each other about, the energy that also *kept* the marriage together might evaporate and the whole thing could come apart like your intestines during a bad bout of Montezuma's revenge. Then it's adios amoebas.

By the way, if you ever break up with someone, destroy all the cards and letters they ever gave you. If you don't, no matter where they are hidden or how ancient—the sender could be dead twenty years—your next spouse will find them. "So, you carried Gloria's books to school, you never carried mine . . ."

But it's not all bad news.

Some couples understand the nature of marriage. They know that a relationship *requires* two people: One to run into the grocery store, and one to sit in the car, look at the time and say, "Oh for crying out loud! You said three items. Let's go!!

See? Some couples can accept and understand what's really important to their partners. They learn how to compromise. For instance, when a friend of mine realized how much it bugged his wife when he left his underwear on the living room floor, he took it off in the kitchen instead.

That's what I call respect.

Arguing is a lot more fun when you're married.

Lots of things can start an argument. A question like, "Are you going to wear your hair like that?" is pretty much the start of a crappy evening for everyone.

A lot of fights begin with the phrase "What's wrong?!"

"Nothing!"

"You set the cat on fire! Don't tell me nothing!"

This is also why most fishing trips began with the phrase "I have had about enough of this shit."

When you're single and you argue, once you're through running each other into the ground there is nothing else to fight about. When you're married, once you get through trashing your partner you can bring a family member into it. No matter how bad you're losing, slamming a relative will turn everything around. You need never lose a fight again.

"Oh yeah? What about your uncle Clark? Last time I checked, nuns' habits were, well . . . for nuns."

If you're behind in the fight, don't hesitate to bring up an unemployed brother or sister with six kids. But remember, once you use these your mom's prison record is fair game.

Lots of times fights happen on the way to family functions. "Oh, jeez, your dad's going to be there. I don't know why we have to do this every year. Your aunt May's gonna be plastered and I bet Aunt June hasn't learned how to chew with her mouth shut yet. The woman's eighty-six years old for goodness sakes. We're going to have to draw straws to see who sits across from her. Last year I got her food all over my face!"

Bringing family into a fight increases the duration by at least eight days. God created the world in less time than it will take for you to kiss and make up. Plus, you're no longer arguing about the topic at hand, you have gone off down an entirely emotional road. This is toughest for the man, who is usually the logical one. (Hey, want to make something of it?) But it's no wonder that taking scatter shots at family hurts. These days most families are the product of divorces and remarriages. It always seems like every time you split the tree, the branch gets a little thinner. For some reason I get the feeling that the Foxworthy tree is suffering from dry rot.

The worst thing a woman can do to a man is nag him in front of his friends. I'm less afraid of slandering someone's family than I am of arguing in public. My wife can pin me to the floor with a butcher knife, but I just want her to wait until we get home. It's even more embarrassing being around a couple when they're fighting.

"Yeah, Tina, why don't you tell them about the time you pushed my mom down the basement stairs."

"They don't want to hear about that."

"Yeah, we would!"

Or say you're on a double date, and they're going at it in the backseat. You don't want to interfere, but after a while something happens that forces you to voice your opinion.

"Jerry, you should have asked me to stop the car before you made Dolores get out. At the least I could have slowed down. You just had to ask."

Too bad we get too old to hit people with a dirt clod when we get mad at them.

Here's something to always remember: When fighting with your wife, never get so mad that you walk out without your keys. I've got a theory that 98 percent of the homeless are people who walked out without their keys and couldn't convince the other party to let them back in.

If fighting persists, divorce, however previously unthinkable, might become an option. But I wonder at how effective a solution dissolution is. After all, isn't divorce when you pay a lawyer a lot of money to arrange it so you can move out and leave everything you own with someone you hate? On the other hand, we can also regard divorce as the legal alternative to murder. In most cases.

It's better just to learn how to avoid arguments. Lots of time women ask questions guys should not answer honestly. My wife always asks me, "Honey, please tell me if my butt starts getting fat."

Yeah, right. I don't care if she's knocking lamps off the table, I'm saying, "You got a really nice butt there, Tundra, I swear you do."

When in public, women should also avoid pointing out other women to their men and asking, "Honey, do you think she's pretty?" She will not get the answer she's looking for. When Gregg does that I always say, "Lord no! Oh, I hate blondes with big firm breasts. I feel lunch coming up. I'm sick as a dog here."

We know better. You'd think she knew better.

Do women really want men to be honest with them on subjects like their hair, clothes, butt, and women on the street? I don't know. But loyalty is a valued quality. For instance, I've never strayed on my wife. No sense in it for lots of good reasons, from my respect and love for Gregg to not wanting to suffocate suddenly in my sleep.

If you're single and dating someone new, you have no idea if the sex game can be won easily or at all. Marriage is more complicated and becomes increasingly so the longer you're together. However, as a married man, your one advantage is knowing that you've won the game before and you've always got a chance to win it again.

Once, I was on the road and I read in *USA Today* that the problem with most men sexually is that they do not spend enough time with their women. We're too wham-bam-thank-you-ma'am, the story said, and women need more than that. Then, unlike most articles that just bash men and leave us to pick up the pieces, this one offered suggestions. Most prominent was to try giving your woman a hot oil massage that lasts an hour. Sounded great until I got to the part that said the whole idea was *never* to touch her in an intimate place. I could go *right up* to the place but I couldn't touch it until the time was up. According to the story, after an hour with the hot oil any woman would be a quivering volcano of passion, ready to erupt.

The night after I got home I told Gregg to just relax. I put the kids to bed. Then, in the privacy of our bedroom, I set up the frying pan and the Coleman stove right by the bed, and warmed up the oil. I put on a romantic CD. I think it was *Mating Dance of the Timberwolf.*

"We're going camping," I said. "You lay back, listen to the music, Daddy's home." Then I did the massage exactly according to instructions. Toes, feet, calves, thighs . . . hey, I'm not going to draw you a picture. Let's just call it all the semimagic spots. I also watched the clock, trying to time things just right. I didn't want to go over the hour mark because the magazine story warned not to try it for longer without supervision. When the hour turned, I looked down hopefully at Gregg. She had her head back and her mouth open. A little drool ran from the corner of her mouth down her cheek. She was fast asleep.

Suddenly the "don't wake me up" rule was in effect.

Damn.

I decided just that once to try and override it. I shook her gently and said, "Hon? You want to . . . ?"

"Oh, I feel too good to do it," she mumbled, somehow knowing what I had in mind even though I hadn't actually mentioned that I was a quivering volcano of passion, ready to erupt. "I couldn't do it. Ohhh, thank you so much. Ohhh, I'll just go to sleep."

She knew I wanted to do it and she just left me hanging.

Maybe she was just concerned about getting oil all over the bed. I didn't care if it was 10-W-40. Besides, I knew it wouldn't go through the paint-covered plastic tarp that I had strategically placed over the mattress. But I had to bite my tongue and not press my no-longer-ulterior motives. So I just put my good deed in the "bank" and said, "Just wanted to make you happy. Didn't care if we did it." Of course, the idea with banking is to be certain to let her know there's something on deposit. All the next day I hinted, "Did you enjoy that hot oil massage? You looked like you enjoyed it. Yeah, I did it for like an hour. Yeah, I could have been doing other things. I don't know, I just love you so much I wanted to do something to make you feel good."

Inside, I couldn't help but wonder how she could say no, particularly when she felt so wonderful. I've never said no to my wife. Actually, there *was* the time I had kidney surgery and was on intravenous morphine. She said I passed on sex—but being semiconscious, it's her word against mine.

One surefire way to tell if a woman feels romantic is if she suddenly starts cleaning the house. I like it when my wife wears the high heels and the little apron. Years ago a woman who liked me sent flowers to get me in a romantic mood. They were nice, but I told her that if she really wanted to push my thrill button she should wash my car.

If a woman wants romance, what might help turn on her man is a visit to the trashy lingerie shop. Or she can just leave her Victoria's Secret catalog lying around. Now, that's never been a big deal with me. I prefer a woman in a T-shirt, white panties, and old Levi's that really fit. I don't need garter belts, corsets, and fishnet stockings. I don't even fit in most garter belts, corsets, and fishnet stockings. I have to think about these things, since I sometimes play dress up when Gregg is out for the afternoon. What man wouldn't? I've just never gotten the hang of all those buttons and snaps.

But that doesn't mean I don't like looking at the pictures in free, home-delivered catalogs of women in their underwear. God bless America. Think about it: We never saw anything like that when we were growing up and needed it. All we ever got was the Sears catalog full of high-waisted granny panties. You could measure first downs with those. "Bring that bra in here, Pete, we gotta take a measurement. First down!"

But that underwear they make now, it's so skimpy that Victoria doesn't have a whole lot of secrets left, does she? You give a couple of guys one of those catalogs and they can entertain themselves all weekend.

"Oh my God, Mike, look at this. That's gotta hurt like hell right there. Just that string going right up your butt like that. Seems like every time you bowled it'd just cut you right in two."

I'll be honest with you: I'd rather look at the catalog than go in their stores. If you're a man, you always feel like a pervert when you're in Victoria's Secret. You do! You feel like the girls behind the counter have the sex offender directory and are just trying to find your picture.

"Sally, look at the guy with the panties on his head. That is the *same* guy." It's gotten so that just because I'm not really a pervert doesn't mean I can't act like one. So every time I go in among the panties and the teddies and the push-up bras, I pick up a body stocking, sashay to the counter, and go, "Where are your dressing rooms." They have to let you try it on. It's the law. Got one on right now, in fact. Little tight in the shoulders, makes it hard to reach all the keys on this keyboard, but it's not really too bad.

There's one question I've never been able to answer: What do women do in the bathroom that takes so long? My wife can be in there six hours, easy. Okay, forty-five minutes, but that's still a long time when there's no shower or bath involved. I go in, shave, brush my teeth, use the facilities, and I'm done in five to seven minutes, tops. The same goes for women and their closets. A man walks into his closet, sees a shirt he likes, smells the pit. Hey, it's okay, and we're out of there. A woman must spin a cocoon.

I suppose one clue to this mystery is a woman's purse. For all her talk of cleanliness, there is nothing a guy has—garage, junk room, fishing box, lint collection—that is more disorganized than a woman's purse. A purse is a dumpster with a shoulder strap. They put garbage in it. They put used Kleenex in there. The put in half-sticks of gum. They put pens that don't write back into the purse. (Buddy Hammond's mom has *ants* in her purse. Wonder why?) The typical purse bottom is so full of spare change it always sets off the metal detectors at airports but not the theft sensors at department stores. Normally having that much metal on one's person would mean a customer *must* be stealing something, but these are women selling to women. They know better.

If my wife dropped her keys in her purse, finding them would make the search for the Holy Grail look like an Easter egg hunt. She thinks she's protected because she's got a can of mace in the purse. That's like protecting your home by keeping a gun somewhere in the attic.

Not a guy in the world has a wallet as disorganized as a woman's purse. Men don't have purses because we'd always lose them, even if they were the size of cars.

As we know, men like things that women don't, like stuffed dead animals on the walls. You never see deer heads in beauty parlors. A sport, to women, is shopping. It really gets them worked up. Here's how I know: "multiple orgasm" and "mall opening" begin with the same letters. Prove it to yourself. Go find a mall under construction and see if at lunchtime there aren't women shouting at the builders to quit eating and get back to work.

Men hate to shop. I guarantee it. Just stop any man you can find and say, "Would you rather spend the whole day shopping for clothes or having exploratory rectal surgery?" Most men would answer quickly: "Now if I had the surgery, how long would I be out of work?"

Clearly there's a world of difference between women and men. Even words mean different things.

When a woman says, "I'm almost ready," a man interprets that to mean "by the year 2000." If you're reading this and that year is already behind us, that still doesn't mean she's ready yet.

Women are always late.

Last year I played for the president at the White House. Sure enough, I looked at my watch, realized we were not ready, and yelled, "Gregg, we're going to be late to meet the president."

"Oh, my hair's not flipping right."

"Nobody will care. Nobody will *know*."

"I'll know. Where's my other earring?"

"This is the White House! Why couldn't this be the one day you were ready twenty minutes early! It's not against the law to sit in the hotel room and watch TV for twenty minutes before we leave."

"Now that I have it on, I don't like this dress."

"Change it."

"Or these shoes." And that's when she starts the flamingo posing, with different shoes on each foot.

"These or these?"

"Let me see it again."

"These or these?"

"Again."

You never see a man with a hunting boot on one foot and a tennis shoe on the other asking which looks better.

"These or these?"

"Let's see that again, Bob."

Sometimes it seems like my whole life with Gregg has been spent running out the door. The problem is that helping my wife get ready also makes me late.

"You got my tie?"

"Yeah, it's in my purse."

"Where's my pants?"

"I don't know. C'mon, c'mon, c'mon."

We always arrive fifteen minutes after everyone else does. Or fifteen minutes after closing time. I was afraid that by the time we got to the White House there'd be a new administration.

Some women in my family will probably be late for their own funerals. The chapel will be full and for some reason the bodies won't be prepped well enough, and we'll all be waiting on them again.

Part of the problem for most women is that they don't know how to calculate driving times. However long it takes to drive somewhere at midnight, with no traffic, going fast, and green lights all the way, is the time they figure it takes to get to the same destination at noon. The fact that it's bumper-to-bumper traffic doesn't come into play. It's still twelve, right? Numbers *look* the same, why shouldn't the driving time be the same? It should always take nineteen minutes to get across town.

Even if a woman can do the math, her *sense* of time is still screwed up. Time is pretty much whatever works for them. Gregg can talk to her mother on the phone for an hour and a half. But if I say, "You've been on the phone for an hour and a half," she'll go, "It's only been half an hour and besides, you talked to your brother last night for forty-five minutes!" Well, I talked to my brother for eleven, but it's not going to help my argument to say so.

Of course, when we're in bed, she goes the other way.

"That was only five minutes."

"No, honey, that was a half an hour."

"No, I looked when we started. It was 11:07, it's 11:12 now and you're finished and smoking."

"No, it was 10:31 when we started."

I suppose in the end, none of this really matters. All I know is that now that I'm married, I always realize right in the middle of sex, "Wow, this is really nice. How could I have forgotten?" This perception is even more intense when you have kids and you have to make an appointment to be intimate. No longer can I think, "Well, if it's not so good tonight, it will be different tomorrow."

Now tomorrow is next week.

So I work really hard at being good in the sack. I want everything to last. But then one of us will move the wrong way and it's over.

"Oh my, I'm sorry, I'm so sorry."

You know it was great sex when you end up apologizing.

Men and women. Husbands and wives. We need each other. Without my wife I wouldn't know what clothes I want to wear or what movies I want to see. I wouldn't have anyone to ask "Where are my socks?" Without me, my wife would have a hard time opening a jar of pickles. She'd also have to buy a bug zapper. "Get it, oooh! It's gross! Smash it, but don't kill it."

With any luck we eventually reach an understanding with each other that allows us to coexist. I don't flush the toilet while she's taking a shower, and she doesn't use the blender while I'm watching *Bass Fishing with Uncle Bullsheets.*

We've lived happily ever after.

The Patter of Little Hooves

A few years ago I became a father. A couple years later the miracle happened again. Now Gregg and I have two young daughters. I thought I knew what I was getting into—at least the second time—but you can't prepare for being a father any more than you can practice loading the entire contents of a four-bedroom house into the trunk of a Buick LeSabre. Believe me, I've tried.

Before Gregg and I got married, she said, "If you want kids, I'm not the person you should marry." I'd wanted kids my whole life. But I was so crazy about her, I was willing not to have kids to be with her.

One morning six years later, Gregg heard a strange ticking. Actually not so strange. We'd had a wild night and she was sleeping on my wristwatch. But later at breakfast she suddenly said, "I want kids." As you can imagine, I was surprised, but Gregg said she was sure, so we immediately began to try—and I do mean immediately. For months nothing happened. So we tried and tried and tried some more. To be perfectly honest, at times I felt I was trying harder than she, but we still kept at it. It's a good thing God made "trying" so much fun.

One Sunday night about ten o'clock, my brother called and said, "Guess what? We're pregnant." We were very happy for Jay, and, naturally, a bit jealous. So that night we tried again. The next morning, right in the middle of making coffee for breakfast, Gregg suddenly said, "You know what? I'm pregnant."

I said, "Get outta here. We only tried last night." (I kicked myself under the table for not having asked her about insanity in the family years ago.)

She said, "I'm telling you, I'm pregnant."

Just to show her that neither my years spent carefully observing the mating habits of farm animals, nor our taxpayer dollars spent on health education in the public schools had been wasted on me, I put down the newspaper, threw on sweatpants, and ran three blocks down the street to the store. I bought two EPT's and came back. She took the test . . . and she was pregnant. She took it again. Same answer. I called my brother. "You're not going to believe this. We're pregnant, too. Yeah, it's great. Oh, listen, while I've got you on the phone, do you know how to get in touch with the people from the *Guinness Book of World Records*?"

After the doctor confirmed the home-test results, we told everyone in the family the good news. When Big Jim found out I was going to be a dad, he just laughed and said, "It's payback time for all the shit you used to do." He was right.

Kids are exactly like marriage and sex in the sense that you can hear other people talk about it, but until you actually do it you have no idea. (Death is the other mystery, but as of now no one's come back to fill us in.) Instead of boring you with the usual heap of platitudes and parental commonsense that you can frankly find in many other books, I'll just pass along the simple advice I give most couples when they're pregnant with their first child.

Sleep.

Let me expand on that. Sleep around the clock. Come home from work and take a nap. Take a nap at work during your lunch hour. Sleep at stoplights and business meetings. Anything will work. You're stockpiling because you're never going to sleep the same or as well for the rest of your life.

To be totally prepared for childbirth, Gregg and I did what all beginner parents do: We took a Lamaze course. I don't know who this Lamaze character is, but the class was chock-full of wonderful tips and stories. One of my favorite moments occurred when the teacher told the group this very important information.

"Now, after your wife's water breaks, do not have sex."

I raised my hand. "Is this really a problem?" I asked. "Are there really men so insensitive?"

The look on her face told me the scary truth: She wouldn't have mentioned this unless someone had actually done it.

"So just how far apart are the contractions there, sweet thang? Seems like a shame to waste this semiprivate room."

It never really struck me that we were having a baby, despite nine months of vomiting and Gregg's stomach the size of Guatemala. I only realized it when the doctor held up my oldest daughter for me to see. (By then she was already two years old and I suddenly understood why everyone had been trying to get my attention.) Seriously, I didn't know that when babies were born they were blue, and that they didn't kick and scream. When I saw her she wasn't moving. I went from that "it hasn't really sunk in" feeling to the "somebody hit you in the stomach with a baseball bat" panic that something was wrong with my kid. The nurses took her over to the table and started working on her, and in a minute I heard "Wahhh."

Only a year after my daughter was born did I tell Gregg what had happened and how I'd felt, and then I just started crying.

Everywhere I go people keep asking me if we videotaped our daughters' births. No, we did not. Got some nice footage of the conception, but nothing on the delivery. I mean, why would anybody want to film that? Because it's such a beautiful moment? I was there. Having a baby looks like a wet Saint Bernard trying to come in through a cat door. Do you really think I need a film to remember this? I think any guy who films his wife giving birth ought to return the favor by letting his wife film his hemorrhoid surgery later.

"Look girls, here's Tony fully dilated. What a trooper he was."

I learned a lot about babies pretty quickly. For instance, babies are nauseated by the smell of a clean shirt. You put on something freshly laundered and they're gonna spit up just like that. My wardrobe looked like we had condors living in our yard. If you play with babies too hard, they'll spew like a can of beer. I used to shake up my daughter, then hand her to people I didn't like. "Hold her just a minute, would ya?"

I also learned that you have *got* to change those diapers every day. You do! When it says ''six to twelve'' pounds on the side of the Pampers box, they're not lying. That is all those things will hold.

Changing a diaper is a lot like opening a birthday present from your grandmother. You never know what's inside, but you're pretty sure you're not going to like it. Changing a diaper after your kid eats a box of Crayolas will stop you dead in your tracks. Looks like a souvenir from Jamaica.

Babies have taught me a few things about moms, too. Moms will clean up anything. I read recently in *Scientific American* that a mother's spit duplicates the exact chemical composition of Formula 409. It can get rust off a car bumper.

I love being a parent. It's weird, it's hard, you sacrifice decades of your life raising someone who, I guarantee you, will one day tell you that you didn't do a damn thing right, and move out in a huff. Next thing you see the kid on *Oprah* blaming you for everything from her mustache to wanting to sleep with his sister (the one with the mustache). I'm getting a little tired of that. Just once I want to see somebody go, ''You know what? My daddy was great, my momma was great, I'm just a jerk.'' Just one time.

People have always told me that I'd learn more from my kids than they'd learn from me. I now believe that. I've learned that as a parent, when you have sex your body emits a hormone that drifts down the hall into your child's room and makes them want a drink of water. If you're extremely lucky they will call this order in, because there are few surprises in life to match looking your wife directly in the eye and feeling somebody tickle the bottom of your foot. So now every night we just bathe the little girls and put them in their nightgowns and their cowbells.

Our youngest child has discovered the little silver handle on the back of the toilet. She's making more stuff disappear than David Copperfield. My wife's lost three combs. I lost my good sunglasses. We're pretty sure she flushed the remote control because every time we go to the bathroom the TV comes on.

Once when I came home from work I discovered that somebody had colored on the dining room wall. My oldest daughter told me the dog did it. I about went crazy. We've had that dog eight years and *now* he starts coloring on the wall.

Between the youngsters and the animals the house just goes to hell. The rule around our place is: If it ain't broke, it ain't ours. They've destroyed everything. My wife has this little statue. It used to be a ballerina, now it just looks like the victim of a tragic farming accident. We have a sofa, but if you sit on it in the wrong place you can't have kids.

Babies today come with technology. Anybody with a baby has a monitor, which for those of you without kids (and who swear after reading this that you will always be without kids), it's like a one-way walkie-talkie that allows you to listen in on them. You have to be real careful to put the right end of this thing in the right bedroom. We realized we'd made that mistake when we didn't hear our daughter cry for five months and her first words were, "Oh yeah baby, just like that, that's really good, that's good . . ."

Anybody with kids knows I'm lying now. When you're young and you've got a choice between sleep or sex, you take sex every time. When you start getting older and you've got a choice between sleep and sex, you take the sleep and just hope you have a dream about sex.

All parents think their kids are the smartest kids ever born. My mom thought my daughter was a genius because she would lie on the floor and talk to the ceiling fan. I said, "Mom, Uncle Harold does that and y'all call him an alcoholic."

It's not that I don't think my daughters are bright. Even if they *are* my kids. (Gregg's got strong genes.) It's just embarrassing to say so out loud because then I sound like every other parent. Who takes these parents seriously anymore? When's the last time you visited someone with little kids who said, "Hey, come in here and look at little Tommy. He is as dumb as a brick, boy. Turn on the light. He won't even know. Turn the light on. He'll just sit there all day long, cross-eyed and drooling."

I have a cousin who thinks her oldest child is going to be the next Einstein because this kid stands out in the yard and goes, "Air'pane. Air'pane."

I finally took her aside and told her. "Listen. He's fourteen years old! It's time to reel it in. I don't want to break your heart, but he's got a job with deep fat frying in his future." I think I may have whispered too loud because a couple of my relatives suddenly said, "Wait a damn minute here."

One thing I *will* brag about is how cute my daughters are. Intelligence is ephemeral, but pictures don't lie. (If you believe that, please put this book on your nightstand next to the copy of *Eleanor Roosevelt: The Supermodel Years*.) I am glad my daughters are comely because frankly I worried about that. Can you think of anything worse than people who have ugly kids? Gregg and I call those unfortunate children "Hi babies" because when you meet a kid so ugly that you can't say anything nice to its parents you say, "Hi, baby."

Parents with "Hi babies" are also always the first ones to whip out their snapshots and shove them in your face. This annoys me so much that when I worked at IBM I got this baby picture that was actually a composite of the ugliest features of forty questionable looking infants. The result was fairly horrible. Whenever guys would start pulling out pictures of their kids, I would dead-serious take out my composite snapshot and go, "That's my son." I just wanted to watch their faces. This "baby" had crossed-eyes, huge ears that didn't match, one eyebrow, one tooth that was directly in the middle, and huge nostrils. People were afraid to say, "That is not your kid," because it might have been. So they'd try to say something nice, and go, "What a cute outfit."

When our oldest child learned to walk we finally had to babyproof the house. You've all heard of this, right? You have to put latches on your drawers and cabinets so your children can't hurt themselves. We don't want them taking knives out of the silverware drawer and playing Ed Aames on the *Tonight Show* anniversary reel.

I remember when I was a kid, my parents had a 900-pound television on top of a TV tray. The Eiffel Tower standing on its point was safer. But my dad's theory was "Let him pull it on his head a few times, he'll learn." He had a similar attitude about sticking metal objects in electrical outlets. "Oh, you want to put a penny in the light socket? Sure. Try that out. Oh, hurt like hell, didn't it? Don't do that no more."

Raising kids is the hardest job in the world. It's a lot like that military commercial: "We do more before 9 A.M. than most people do all day." That's our household. Now we look back and realize why we suddenly stopped seeing our friends who'd had kids. We thought we'd done something wrong. The truth was, they'd moved on. They had a responsibility that could not be ignored or even postponed. You can change jobs and spouses and houses, but you can't change your kids.

I read in the newspaper about someone who got in trouble for trying to lose his kids in a mall. Obviously he didn't know that the law only allows you to do that with your wife.

Now that we're parents we are on the other end of the equation. We used to have single friends, but not anymore. We miss them, but we understand that single people don't want to sit around and hear our conversations about birthday parties, car pools, and the preschool staff. My single guy friends are interested in *dating* the cute kindergarten teacher. The dads I know just want her to watch their kids so they can take a nap. Single people want to talk about things other than tinkle and poo-poo and pee-pee. We college-educated parents would also like that, but you'd be amazed at how "doody" has become a sizable part of our vocabulary.

As our kids grow, they've also adopted *our* terminology. Gregg and I have a code phrase for having to go to the bathroom. "I'm going to go check the mildew on the shower curtain." Recently our four-year-old walked into our bedroom and said, "Mom, I think I'm gonna go check the mildew."

Gregg said, "Where did she get that from?"

I just looked at her and said, "Where do you think?"

Gregg did a double take then said, "Oh she's *so* smart." Just like a parent.

Sometimes when I help around the house Gregg really appreciates it. Not only will she shower me with praise but she'll tell her girlfriends.

"Oh, he fed the girls dinner and he's bathing them now."

"He bathes the girls?!"

"Oh yeah, he bathes them every night."

Unfortunately, those friends then tell their husbands.

"Robert, do you know that Jeff bathes their kids every night?"

Soon I'm getting angry calls giving me a hard time for making the guys' lives miserable.

"Thanks a lot, you sonofabitch. I got railed on for a week because you bathe your kids."

All my oldest daughter wants to do from the moment she gets up is play. I wish she'd learn to tell time already so she wouldn't wake me up so early to play with her. But that said, all I really want for her is to enjoy this time of life since it's the *only* time she'll get to play so freely. What would be nice is if life worked the other way around. When we retire we should all get to sit on the floor and play, and not just in senior homes.

As a dad, I'm a pretty good playmate considering that I get tired after about twenty minutes of fooling around with Legos or my daughter's pocket puppies. I don't mean to complain. Playing with those is actually easier than trying to keep up with a kid's imagination. Plus, my scenarios are always a little more gross than Gregg's.

"Oh, Winnie the Pooh ate too much honey. Bluh, he vomited all over Tigger!"

Gregg will roll her eyes, but my daughter loves it.

She is an interesting child. She likes accident stories.

When I put her to bed at night I normally say, "We're going to read a couple of stories." Her eyes light up and she says, "Then we'll tell accidents?"

"Okay."

"Dad, tell me a frog accident."

Then I have to make up a bad accident that happens to a frog. "Frog went out to play; he was jumping, chasing a butterfly, and he bumped his head against the tree."

"No, Daddy, it's got to be a better accident than that."

Then I have to come up with something involving stitches or a cast or dismemberment. Frog parts winding up in a French restaurant is always good, although there should be a happy ending, if possible, like "and he tasted very much like chicken." I've now struck a deal with her that she's got to tell me one accident story for every one I tell her. She's getting pretty good at it.

"Okay, Daddy, the bird was flying in the air and he ran into a giraffe, and his beak poked the giraffe in the eye and the giraffe had to go to the hospital. They put a patch on it and they thought he was going to be blind. But after a few weeks the rhinoceros doctor took the patch off and the giraffe could see, and his mother was so happy."

Just to keep this from being a totally bizarre and sick experience that is guaranteed to make her need therapy, Gregg and I use the stories to teach her important lessons like not going into the street.

"Dad, tell me a rabbit accident."

"There was a rabbit named Donny. One day he wanted to go play with his friend across the street, but Donny didn't always mind his mother and daddy and he didn't stop, look, and listen. Donny hopped into the street and just then a big truck ran over him and crushed his legs. The bones were sticking out."

Just trying to get my point across.

We have a doctor friend who visited recently and she loved the accident stories so much that she actually wrote a kids' book. My daughter described the accidents and our friend Jane wrote them down and did illustrations.

"Okay, there were two cows and one's name was Yakky and the other one's name was Shoe-new. Shoe-new was not a nice cow and would stab Yakky in the stomach with his horn. One day Yakky died and Shoe-new was so mean, he died too." We always try to include a moral to the story. For instance, "Never stab your friends in the stomach with your horns."

We now have a book full of accident stories that the insurance companies would love to get their hands on. We're saving this for when she grows up. It will also come in handy as a discipline tool should she turn out to be a difficult teen.

"You'd better straighten up, young lady, because we've got all we need *right here in this book* to send you away to a girls' school for the rest of your life!"

A kid's job is to drive his parents crazy.

I like to think of my childhood as a job well done.

My mom was always "having a nervous breakdown." Sometimes she'd say we were giving her a brain tumor. Seems like she's had one since we were four. We think the tumor is mobile. Sometimes it's on the left side of the head, sometimes it's on the back. I just thank God that in thirty-three years it's never become fatal.

Too bad Carole was never much good at discipline. She couldn't hurt you when she whipped you. She would *think* she hurt you, but we never really felt it. That's when I first learned how to act.

"Oh God, Mother, stop. Oh, oh, I'm just about to pass out."

"You are not."

"Then I will surely bleed from these welts."

It was all I could do not to laugh. Whether she used her hand, a belt, or a switch, she didn't have it in her heart to spank hard. I remember one time she whipped me and my sister, Jenny. Afterward we started up the stairs and broke into laughter. My dad heard it and told us to come back down. Nobody laughed the next time up the stairs. Big Jim could wear out your ass. He was like a gunslinger. He could do that Magic Dad thing, where he'd hold his hands at his side, reach, unbuckle his belt, pull it off and have it doubled over in one hand in less than two seconds.

Nowadays you can't spank your children in front of other people, which is why my wife and I stay home all the time. Seriously, I guess they have to implement these rules for the people who go overboard. We have to be concerned. But I certainly don't think a swat scarred me. Look at how normal I am! Most of us grew up with corporal punishment. Now it's a time-out. You go sit in your room with the door closed. Tough life. That's what I *wanted* to do.

"Oh darn, I've got to go sit in my room for five minutes. Maybe I better check out these toys. They look lonely."

Don't get me wrong. I'd rather not whack the kid on the bottom. Only once. Lightly. As if a gentle breeze were wafting by. When I have to, I feel bad about it. Our parents were right: It hurts them more than it hurt us. My fingers *always* sting for a few minutes.

Kids think nothing of manipulating their parents. It's just another line in their job description. When I put my daughter to bed I tell her we're going to read two books. As we start on the second she will say, "You know, Daddy, I love you soooooo much. Can we read *three* books tonight?"

"All right, three books."

Three hours later I've got on my heavy coat and I'm just coming back from the public library.

If there are two parents present, the kid will play them off each other. They figure out which parent they're most in trouble with and then they cozy up to the other. Of course, as a parent you've got to take advantage of that love whether it's real or not.

"Damn right your mother's crazy. It's you and me, honey."

When a child wants something their most effective tool is whining. I don't know a parent who would not take a million dollars for their four-year-old after a trip down the cereal aisle at the supermarket. It's like running the gauntlet: shooting the rapids and squealing like a pig. What's worse is that by four they already know all the cereal brands—especially the sugared varieties—as well as the jingle tunes. If only they'd one day pay that much attention to their homework.

Kids whine when they don't get something they want.

"Can I have a Popsicle?"

"No, it's before dinner."

"Wahhh . . ."

You get so sick so quick that you give in. You're not supposed to, but they wear you down. It's like basic training.

I think adults should employ this technique more often. Why give it up just because you've left childhood behind?

"You know, John, I only like you as a friend."

"Wahhh . . . I don't want you to like me as a friend, I want you to sleep with me one time . . ."

"But . . ."

"Wahhh."

"Okay. Alright. Once! One time I'll sleep with you."

All new parents eventually realize that they are just like their own parents, only, they hope, different. All those things that we swore when we were thirteen years old that we were never going to say to our children, just blurt from our mouths. Then we look in the mirror and think, "Oh my God, I just said 'Because I said so.' I can't believe I said that."

But I also found that as soon as I had kids, I appreciated my own parents a lot more. I started calling my mom and dad regularly. Suddenly I understood the sacrifices they had made. Not only financially, but timewise. Just between wiping my butt and my nose and changing my clothes, they spent a lot of man/woman hours getting me grown.

The number one parent complaint in the world is "I never have any time for myself." Why is this? Simple. All our lives we've been given bad information. Since we were five years old, we've been told, "Don't act like a baby. Don't act like a kid." I think if you *would* act like a kid you could have a lot of time to yourself. Say you're introduced to somebody you've never met before. Act like a kid. Put your finger in your nose. You never have to worry about this person calling you, writing to you, or wanting to spend time with you again. Go to somebody's house and jump on the bed. He'll never invite you back. Tell your boss you can't work and that you're scared because there's a monster in the break room. You're going to have plenty of time for yourself until your unemployment runs out.

Before we were married, Gregg and I used to sit around in the morning and read the paper over breakfast. Before we had kids, I loved it when Gregg could come back to bed in the morning after feeding the pets, and it was playtime. Now I love it when my wife gets up with the baby and lets me sleep.

Kids change everything. Now when we drive down the street and Gregg sees a billboard with a woman wearing a bikini, she will say, "Honey, I used to look like that before I had kids."

So I will say, "That's *why* you had kids, honey."

Women are never happy with their bodies afterward. Men should probably have kids because we don't care about how we look the same way women do. Stretch marks on our butts? We never *look* at our butts. There's not a guy in the world who looks at his posterior—or will admit it. I just assume it's there because my pants haven't fallen down.

I learned something about men's butts when my wife sent my brother and me to the Atlanta Braves Fantasy Camp for Christmas, where guys get to live out their major league dream and play with the real players. It cost $3,500, and you have to be at least thirty to go. Most of the guys were doctors and lawyers. Most were also between fifty and sixty years old. At the end of the week one of the Braves asked me "Did you learn anything?"

I said, "Yes, I did. I have learned there is nothing uglier than an old man's ass." Looks like somebody hung a bean bag chair over a clothesline. I suppose this is inevitable. Unlike our wives', our butts don't get fat. The bottom half just disappears. It's like an alien ass. I've never seen an alien ass, but I'm assuming that's what one would look like. You can't look at one and not shudder, I know that for a fact. When I walked through that locker room, every BA I'd ever flashed came back to haunt me. The only thing worse that I've ever seen was my grandmother naked. Purely by accident. I will remember that vision until the day I die. Weeks later I'd still get full-body shivers. Nothing was in the right place. She looked like a bloodhound in a shower cap. I thought about it for a while and I decided it was God getting even with me for all the times in my life I tried to see women naked.

"Hey, Jeff, you want to see naked women? Huh? Here's your grandma!"

The hardest part of Fantasy Camp was accepting how out of shape we were. Guys could still hit. Some could still throw a little bit. But nobody could run any more. You hit it to the wall and it'd be a bang-bang play at first. When I was seventeen my fantasy involved two redheads and a gallon of Cool Whip. When I first arrived at camp, my fantasy was to hit a triple. After four days my fantasy was to put my socks on by myself. Everybody was so sore. After two days the hotel sounded like a brothel. I'd walk down the hall and hear guys in their rooms going, "Ooo. OOO. OOOOO."

"Hey, you got a girl in there?"

"No, I'm just taking my shirt off. Now I'm brushing my teeth."

Onstage I talk about my vasectomy. This is not something I just invented to be funny, although sometimes I wish it were.

Before I got the procedure, I had to get counseling. The doctors think it's a good idea. They want to make sure you know what you're doing. Somehow, I don't think dropping your pants for some guy with a razor is an impulse decision.

I didn't really want to do it. Like all guys I thought, "What if I want to have another family? You might call that a tradition with the Foxworthys. Or what if Gregg got hit by a bus tomorrow? Then I'd need to marry a gorgeous twenty-year-old and start all over again. Or I might get really adventurous and become one of those weird guys who have whole families in different towns and manage to split their time between both by telling their wives they are traveling for business.

"Gonna be on the road for half our married life, if it's okay with you, dear."

Of course, the idea of my vasectomy didn't bother Gregg a bit. After two difficult pregnancies, she was all for it. She was properly sympathetic about what I was about to endure, but not about my other fears because the doctors had assured me that in most cases the procedure was reversible. Yeah right. All I need is to be forty-nine and have Gregg suddenly say, "I need another baby," and not be able to answer the call.

Now that it's a done deal, a friend told me that the only way to handle the dark wellspring of this mortifying trauma that still haunts me is to share my experience.

"Talk about it," she said, "One day you'll get over it." So I use it in my act. It's painful, but not as painful as listening to other men tell me stories that make me want to live in a deer stand for the rest of my life.

Here it is. You lie on a cold, stainless steel table. You're not wearing pants. Right where you can see it—who's sick idea is that?—is a tray with a razor, a hook, a soldering iron, and two large syringes. My brother-in-law, Richard, told me that when he got his cords cut, they used the soldering iron and discovered it wasn't grounded.

The words "torture implements" and "no pants" don't even belong in the same sentence. When I asked a friend about his vasectomy, he only got as far as the word "razor" before I felt a sudden pain in my package. I looked down and realized I had crossed and squeezed my legs together tighter than a torqued bolt. You could hold a million dollars in front of a guy and say, "I'll give you all the money if you can just sit with both feet on the floor and listen to how it's done," and you'd never lose a penny. It's just not possible. Even after the operation is complete and you've healed, reached retirement age, and started collecting Social Security, you're never over the terror.

The anesthetic is local, though it seemed long distance to me. I got a shot in both sides of my scrotum to numb it. (The memory is so painful that it took me ten minutes just to type out the preceding sentence.) Meanwhile, I tried to make small talk with a doctor who reminded me of Buddy Hammond making his mom a change purse, while he kept talking about country music.

"Hey, you know who I really like?"

"Somebody with a high voice, I assume."

I didn't really feel the first shot. The second hit a nerve. That hurt so much that when I got home I couldn't even use the remote control. Then my equipment went into hiding. I had to stick my finger up my butt and holler "Snake!" just to pee.

The operation is also embarrassing. For some reason, there's a nurse in the room. I kept hoping she wouldn't look at me. There is better-looking plumbing in the newborn room at the hospital.

The preop instructions say you have to bring a jockstrap with you. When you're done, they pack the front full of gauze. I looked like Tom Jones in concert. Walking from the doctor's office to the car, I got invited to three proms.

"Leave me alone, my wife's waiting on me."

While recovering I actually wanted to call people and get them to look at my bruises of many colors. No body part has ever been these colors before: yellow, green, mauve, taupe, black, purple. But don't try to get any sympathy from your buddies. They always say, "Oh, it doesn't really hurt." They're lying. But pretty soon you're telling the same lie. The reason is that if you were dumb enough to fall for the whole deal, you want to get somebody else to fall for it.

The good thing was that when the pain *really* went away I felt like a sixteen-year-old. For the first time in my sexual life I didn't have to worry about getting somebody pregnant. When my wife said, "The baby's taking a nap," I said, "Hey, the baby's taking a nap! Perhaps you and I should take a nap."

"Get away from me with that thing."

Damn. Got a new one and can't even use it.

Of course, there's a good reason to endure such embarrassment and pain. The alternatives are worse. I'm not talking about unwanted children. You always want them. But other preventive methods make spontaneity fly out the window. IUD's are a hassle.

The pill causes some women to vomit pea soup, like Linda Blair in *The Exorcist*. I've got no problem with women hurling, but I hate it when the bed levitates halfway to the ceiling.

Contraceptive foam is the pits. That stuff is almost as effective as the pill yet it contains no ingredient that actually prevents pregnancy. The way it works is this: When you're finished making love and you go to pee, it burns so bloody awfully that you feel like the star client at your local VD clinic. I felt as if I were engulfed in flames. Suddenly I didn't want to have sex for another six months. When you only do it twice a year, the chance of conception is very low.

Six weeks after the vasectomy operation you're supposed to take in a sample to the doctor. Then wait four months and take another. They give you two little cups to use. Someone knowing what you're *really* doing in the bathroom takes all the thrill away. It's humiliating, taking the cup into the doctor's office and announcing to a full waiting room, "Hey, here's my sperm sample." I suppose it could have been worse. I might have had to do it in a little room at the doctor's. How much time is appropriate to spend summoning the sample? If you're back in forty seconds, they'll talk about you. If you're gone an hour, they'll talk about you. Maybe I should have stayed an hour and then when I came out, said, "Sorry, the first four weren't perfect, so I threw them away."

I don't feel that terrible about not having more kids. I used to want a son, bad, but it might be tough being my son. I'd relive all my sports fantasies and make his life miserable. I'd want him to be a football star and I'm afraid that at halftime, when all the other dads go to get hot chocolate, I'd be saying, "Sorry, fellas, I've got to stay. Eugene's got a baton solo tonight."

I worry about my daughters, too. I spent the first half of my life trying to get into girls' knickers and I'm going to spend the rest of my life trying to keep other guys out of theirs.

Hey, cut it out. This is no laughing matter.

When Cousins Marry

I believe in the family. I've always told stories about my relations and even used them as the inspiration for a Redneck joke or two . . . hundred. Without their example to draw on I might still be doing stand-up over Kroger's intercom and checking stock in the backroom between ''sets.''

I'm feeling kind of grateful and spiritual now, so I'd like to share with you what family means to me.

Your family is a pack of idiots whom you have to love. We exist on earth to love each other, and our family is the test. Family is different from friends. You can pick your friends. It's easy to love your friends, *because* you pick them. But with family, God just sorts through the whole pile of souls and says, "This one will hate this one—okay, they're brothers. This one will drive everyone crazy—she'll be the aunt." You just get stuck with these people, and most of them are nuts. You let family get away with behavior you wouldn't put up with from your closest friends, let alone strangers. You love your family and hate them, fight with and fight for them. But in the end they're all you've got.

There are no secrets in my family. It's not that we don't try to keep them, it's just that my kin are the biggest bunch of blabber-mouths in the world. To say, "Don't tell anybody I told you this," is to waste your breath. You might as well rent the Goodyear blimp and advertise.

"Don't tell anybody I told you this, but the girl Cousin Jerry's dating is four months' pregnant." Before the sun has set, some relative from Alaska will call and say, "We hear Jerry's dating a girl with a hunchback and three six-year-olds."

In my family they don't even try to get it right.

The family reunion is your annual reminder about how weird your relations really are. Uncle Leonard has a bumper sticker on his bowling ball and is still upset that *Gunsmoke* was canceled. Aunt Ida is the state's only female Elvis impersonator. Cousin Joanie's talent in the local beauty pageant was making noises with her arm-pit. Her brother, Bradley, can eat a McDonald's double cheese-burger in one bite. And what about Grandma, who starts every day by asking, "Anyone seen my teeth?" The notion that these people swim in the same gene pool as you is enough to make you quit dating your second cousin and stop calling your van the "Love Machine."

On the other hand, some people look forward to family reunions, especially those who hope they will get to go after the parole board finally meets.

My maternal grandmother's family, the Sheats, always holds their reunions at a campground on the south side of Atlanta. When I was a kid, everyone wore their Sunday best. The adults sang church songs while the kids played football. We'd always tear something, but the beating was still worth not having to sing.

My grandfather Camp's family was also big on reunions, but that was because they all lived to be over a hundred years old. By then these folks didn't have much to look forward to *but* the reunion and that time of day when the prunes kicked in. Fortunately they were funny people, though considering their advanced age and their digestive systems, they had to be very careful how hard they laughed.

The Foxworthy clan didn't get together very often for reunions because our gatherings always ended in fights. Once we had all the relatives come down to Big Jim's farm for the weekend. For a while things went well. Then we decided to go to a hayfield for a family softball game. This game included a couple of cousins, Ben and Richard, that Big Jim had never much liked. In the middle of the third inning my brother, Jay, slid into second base and Cousin Ben tagged him too hard, I guess. Big Jim was up next. When he got to second base, he threw a big hairy forearm at Ben. Next thing, everyone was brawling in the middle of the baseball diamond. Somehow I'm certain that God looked down on that spectacle and thought, "Why did I give these people the ability to reproduce?"

It would take four or five years just for hurt feelings to heal enough so that everyone could talk again. Suddenly the attitude would be, "Come on, come on, live and let live. Let bygones be bygones. They're family!" Then we'd have another reunion and there'd be another fight.

Occasionally the Foxworthy side and the Sheats/Camp side would meet, mostly at weddings. Unfortunately, the spirit of love was usually confined to the lucky couple, since Carole's family didn't much care for Big Jim, for obvious reasons. However, Big Jim and my grandfather James Camp still fished together all the time. They'd leave at five in the morning, after my granddaddy had already worked a full shift. My dad said he learned how to drive when he was tired on those trips. My granddaddy's method was to pick something really far down the road, like a telephone pole, and then just sleep until he got to it. I remember riding to the farm with Big Jim and desperately trying to make small talk because I knew that otherwise he'd fall asleep. He hit a deer once. We were going about eighty. The impact woke him up, the car spun a 360 but managed to stay on the road. Unfortunately, the collision destroyed all the meat and we were really disappointed. I mean, what's a car bumper worth when you're talking about dinner for twelve?

There were some interesting people in Big Jim's mother's family, the Abstances. The one I remember most was Uncle Joe, a preacher. At one reunion, when I was in high school, I had already started to do imitations, like of the Reverend Billy Graham. At the gathering my brother kept saying, "Hey, do Billy Graham!"

It went something like this: "Well *you* know, people ask me, 'Billy, is premarital sex bad?' and I would say, 'Pray about it—no, wait, I tell you, premarital sex does not *have* to be bad. It all depends on who . . . you . . .' "

That's when Uncle Joe threw a glass of tea in my face. I stopped the imitation right then and there—until Uncle Joe left, and then I did it some more.

One of my favorite family members was Uncle Sid. He could always make me laugh. Uncle Sid was funny not only in life but also in death. He passed away at the ripe old age of ninety-two. When I went to pay my final respects, I found Uncle Sid lying in his coffin, decked out in his best blue suit. He had a button on his lapel that read, "Who farted?"

A funeral is really a family reunion minus one.

I may have a family of crazies, but there's also a select handful who don't include themselves in the seriously afflicted group. We intentionally do stupid stuff with a wink to each other. We're just kidding. The rest of them *really* need help.

For instance, my brother and I have a tradition. All our lives we have told each other what we're getting the other for Christmas the minute we buy it. My brother will come home from the mall and call me, and say, "You want to know what I'm getting you for Christmas?"

"Yeah."

"I got you a sweatshirt."

"Yeah? What kind?"

"Florida State."

"Oh, cool. What color?"

"Maroon. What'd you get me?"

"Oh, blah blah blah."

Then, when the family gets together to open the Christmas presents, my brother will hand me mine and go, "Here's your gift, Jeff, from me." Then he'll pause and say, "If you could have anything in the whole world, what would it be?"

I'll say, "God, anything in the whole world? You know what I'd really love? I'd love a sweatshirt."

"What kind of sweatshirt?"

"A Florida State sweatshirt."

"What color?"

"Maroon."

This is usually when someone in the family finally remembers what we do and says, "Dammit, you boys are doing it again."

The family's covered dish Christmas party was always potluck. Everyone made something at home that they were especially proud of and brought it in a casserole dish. After some of the reactions these concoctions got as they were passed around the dinner table, I've wondered why the cooks remain so fond of their creations. My mother can't go anywhere without making a congealed salad. It's as if a bowl of Jell-O hit a can of Del Monte Fruit Cocktail at eighty miles an hour, then sat out on the roadside for a week. Adults will eat this stuff, but the kids just spend all their time picking out the fruit. One of my aunts cooks the green beans covered with "something." You scrape off the "something," save it to grease your car, and eat the beans.

I always looked forward to seeing my uncle Jimmy at the party. He was a real character.

About fifteen years ago he was shopping in one of those warehouse outlet suit stores and found the ugliest suit of all time. It was double knit, with huge lapels and giant bell bottoms, and all in bright red with black-and-white checks.

The suit was on sale, of course, and Jimmy, sensing a bargain, bought it. Jimmy's a big man; probably six four, 250 pounds. For somebody that large to wear something that awful just made the sight of him walking down the street even more horrible. Still, one of the major attractions each year at the Christmas party was to see if Uncle Jimmy would wear his suit.

About four or five years ago the party was at Uncle Jimmy's house. When we arrived, he answered the door. He wore the suit jacket, but not the pants. I bummed out on the spot. All I could say was, "Jimmy, what happened to the pants?"

"I had to stop wearing them," he said.

"Are they damaged?"

"Nope."

"Then why?"

"They went out of style."

I've got a bet with my brother that the jacket won't go out of style before the pants come back in.

The most fun I've ever had at a covered dish Christmas dinner was when I followed my aunt Dolores around and watched her work her special magic with an item called "fake vomit." This gag played best if associated with a recipe someone always bragged about. It wasn't the fake vomit that was particularly funny. In fact, it was disgusting in a latex sort of way. The best moments were Aunt Dolores' wonderful sound effects and profuse apologies. I laughed so hard I was afraid I'd soil my undergarments. Every time I heard her proclaim, "It must have been that long car ride, that's all I can think of," I would snort like a pig and have to run out of the room. What amazed me even more than Aunt Dolores' thespian talents was that the trick worked year after year after year. I guess people just don't file vomit in the long term memory column.

The holidays are a time for giving and sharing; it's a time when love is in the air. Literally.

As a joke, my brother used to hang a pair of panty hose over his fireplace before Christmas. He said that all he wanted was for Santa to fill them. What they say about Santa checking the list twice must be true because every Christmas morning, although Jay's kids' stockings overflowed, his poor panty hose hung sadly empty and grew increasingly threadbare.

One year I decided to make his dream come true. I put on sunglasses and a fake beard and went in search of an inflatable love doll. Of course, they don't sell those things at Wal-Mart. I had to go to an adult bookstore downtown. If you've never been in an X-rated store, don't go. You'll only confuse yourself. I was there almost three hours saying things like, "What does that do?" "You're kidding me!" "Who owns that?" "Do you have their phone number?"

Finally, I made it to the inflatable doll section. I wanted to buy a standard, uncomplicated doll suitable for a night of romance that could also substitute as a passenger in my truck so I could use the car pool lane during rush hour. I'm not sure what a complicated doll is. Perhaps one that is subject to wild mood shifts and using a French accent for no reason at all. (That also describes a few ex-girlfriends.) Finding what I wanted was difficult. Love dolls come in many different models. The top of the line, according to the side of the box, could do things I'd only seen in a book on animal husbandry. I figured the ''vibro-motion'' was a feature Jay could live without, so I settled on Lovable Louise. She was at the bottom of the price scale. To call Louise a ''doll'' took a huge leap of imagination.

On Christmas Eve, with the help of an old bicycle pump, Louise came to life. My sister-in-law was in on the plan and cleverly left the front door key hidden under the mat. In the wee morning hours, long after Santa had come and gone, I snuck into the house and filled the dangling panty hose with Louise's pliant legs and bottom. I also ate some cookies and drank what remained of a glass of milk on a nearby tray. Then I let myself out, went home, and giggled for a couple of hours.

The next morning my brother called to say that Santa had been to his house and left a present that had made *him* very happy but had left the dog confused. He would bark, start to walk away, then come back and bark some more. I suggested he purchase an inflatable Lassie to set Rover straight. We also agreed that Louise should remain in her panty hose so the rest of the family could admire her when they came over for the traditional Christmas dinner. It seemed like a great idea, except that we forgot that Grandma and Grandpa would be there.

My grandmother noticed Louise the moment she walked in the door. ''What the hell is that?'' she asked. My brother quickly explained.

''It's a doll.''

"Who would play with something like that?" Granny snapped. I had several candidates in mind, but I kept my mouth shut. "Where are her clothes?" Granny continued. I hadn't seen any in the box, but I kept this information to myself.

"Boy, that turkey sure smells nice, Gran," Jay said, trying to steer her into the dining room. But Granny was relentless.

"Why doesn't she have any teeth?"

Again, I could have answered, but why would I? It was Christmas and no one wanted to ride in the back of the ambulance saying, "Hang on Granny, Hang on!"

My grandfather, a delightful old man with poor eyesight, sidled up to me and said, "Hey, who's the naked gal by the fireplace?" I told him she was Jay's friend. A few minutes later I noticed Grandpa by the mantel, talking to Louise. Not just talking, but actually flirting. Sadly, he thought he was doing well. It was then that we realized this might be Grandpa's last Christmas at home.

The big dinner went well. We made the usual small talk about who had died, who was dying, and who should be killed, when suddenly Louise made a noise that sounded a lot like my father in the bathroom in the morning. Then she lurched from the panty hose, flew around the room twice, and fell in a heap in front of the sofa. The cat screamed, I passed cranberry sauce through my nose, and Grandpa ran across the room, fell to his knees, and began administering mouth to mouth resuscitation. My brother wet his pants and Granny threw down her napkin, stomped out of the room, and sat in the car. It was indeed a Christmas to treasure and remember.

Later in my brother's garage, we conducted a thorough examination to decide the cause of Louise's collapse. We discovered that Louise had suffered from a hot ember to the back of her right thigh. Fortunately, thanks to a wonder drug called duct tape we restored her to perfect health. Louise went on to star in several bachelor party movies. I think Grandpa still calls her whenever he can get out of the house.

Thanksgiving is also a magical day. One reason is that in my family we get to try out the same food we'll eat a month later at the covered dish Christmas party. Another is that we get a pretty good idea of how much antacid we should stock up on.

Thanksgiving is the way in which families spread hundreds of miles apart can be united. We share an afternoon and a bountiful meal, and soon enough hours have passed to remind us why we moved do far apart from each other in the first place. Then we all pile into our minivans and head back to our respective castles. The drive home is a wonderful opportunity to reflect with our spouses about who looked fat and how out of control their children were. We should stop to think about how wrong it is to judge others, but we don't, especially when we realize how quickly this conversation makes the drive fly by.

Being grateful on Thanksgiving isn't limited to only that year's blessings. It's okay to give thanks for how lucky you are on Thanksgiving itself. For example, you can give thanks:

• For healthy, new babies and new in-laws (some prayers are more sincere than others).

• That you didn't have to sit across the table from Uncle Lou again, a man who loves to talk, yet doesn't like to wear his false teeth.

• That your home football team didn't play on Turkey Day, so you don't have to feel bad about sleeping through the second half.

• That your grandmother told the story about the time she went to church in two different colored shoes only fourteen times.

• That your cousin Mark didn't ask you for a job again this year.

• That Uncle Bob washed his kids instead of his car for a change.

• That Aunt Dorothy brought cake instead of that crappy dressing of which she's so proud.

• That Uncle Tom finally got his hearing aid repaired.

• That Uncle Tom's hearing aid batteries went dead just when you called him a no count *%$#*.

• That your cousin's new wife didn't wear a bra.

• That Grandpa hit your brother's car instead of yours.

• That to Uncle Frank, whom you see only at this time of year, you still don't have to say anything more than "Can you move your car so I can get out."

• That your mom finally got the dishwasher repaired and has stopped using the dog in its place.

• That your dad's video camera broke early in the day, so you didn't have do that stupid "smile and wave" all afternoon.

• That this year dinner was at your brother's house instead of Aunt Jessie's, which always smells like a combination of mildew and cold cream.

• That Cousin Doug for once couldn't make it. His habit of staring and licking his lips makes everyone uncomfortable.

• That on the first Thanksgiving the Pilgrims chose turkey instead of Spam.

• That today's dinner was not too slow crossing the highway yesterday.

Amen.

This is a true story. A couple of years ago I did something I'd always wanted to do. I cashed in all my frequent-flier miles and took everybody in my family to Hawaii. Thirteen people. I thought it would be the vacation of a lifetime. It ended up being *The Clampetts Go to Maui.*

If you can actually gather my family all in one place at the same time, I guarantee you there's an empty K Mart somewhere. They showed up at the airport with coolers and grocery bags for luggage. The skycap asked my cousin Fred, "Which one's yours, the Samsonite?"

"No, we got the Igloo with the duct tape on it and the five Piggly Wiggly bags right there."

At the ticket counter I asked my mother, "Mom, would you like to sit next to the window?"

She said, "Oh, I better not, I just had my hair fixed."

The movie they showed was *Homeward Bound: The Incredible Journey*. Five minutes after it began my brother turned to me and said, "You know that ain't them dogs' real voices." Then my sister got mad: "Well thanks for spoiling it for everybody else!"

In Maui we stayed right on the beach. From our hotel room balconies we could see whales migrating. They came right up out of the water. That first morning my brother was more excited about this natural wonder than I'd ever seen him excited about anything.

"Boy, I wish I had a gun with a scope on it," he said. "Anyone know how much it costs to mount a whale? I'd have to get a bigger trailer, I tell you that."

You could tell which rooms were ours from the underwear hanging off the railings. Our hotel also became the site of the only peeing-for-distance contest ever held in Maui. I am ashamed to say my aunt Rose won in the second round. I don't believe the hotel minded, though. They now include a little write-up about the contest in their advertising brochure.

I started to wonder whether I should have taken my family so far from home when my uncle Doug kept asking, "When we gonna convert our money to Hawaiian money?"

Later we went to a luau. After we finished the pig, they asked for volunteers to do the hula. Doug raised his hand. Halfway through the dance we all realized Doug wasn't wearing any Skivvies underneath his hula skirt. When we asked him about it later, he said, "Well, when I went to put that skirt on I noticed I had a hole in my drawers and I didn't want to embarrass myself."

Got to give him credit for thinking it out, though.

I love my family anyway. They're good people. They just don't get out much, mainly because of that no shirt–no shoes rule. They loved that hotel, though. They stole everything they could. They swiped the ashtrays while we were *checking in*. Didn't even dump the sand out of them. One morning I had to dry myself off with toilet paper after my shower because my cousin had stuffed all the towels in a Piggly Wiggly bag. When the maid made the mistake of taking her lunch break and leaving her cart out in the hall, the family was on that like a pack of dogs on a three-legged cat. Picked it clean. Later I asked my brother, "What are you going to do with 180 shower caps?"

"Christmas presents," he said. Then his wife got mad: "Well thanks for spoiling it for everybody else!"

On the way back from Hawaii the family spent a few days with Gregg and me in Los Angeles. I took them to the La Brea tar pits to see the prehistoric fossils. My brother said, "Man, just don't seem like dinosaurs would come this close to downtown, does it?" I'm not making this up, I swear. It's just my bloodline.

As I said good-bye to everyone at the airport, I started thinking that my family must be the biggest bunch of goobers in the whole world. By the time we'd been together only a week I'd already had fantasies about being adopted. Maybe I had a normal family that was desperately trying to find me. I imagined that they were financially secure, morally sound, and lived to love and support each other. Then I realized there is no such thing as a sane, functional family.

The more I thought about it the more I understood that families are like chameleons. They can put on a good face and fool the outside world. However, put them all in the same house for a long weekend and they fall apart like a papier mâché bathtub. It's because everyone in the family knows everyone else's weaknesses and will gladly exploit them for the sake of an argument or for a good laugh. Addictions, unemployment, and undesirable physical features are all fair game where loved ones are concerned. If someone doesn't cry, throw a punch, or leave, it can't really be considered a family get-together can it? Each outing with loved ones should produce another level of emotional scarring for at least someone present. This in turn helps to feed the economy through the purchase of therapy sessions, self-help books, and alcohol. I think if families were well adjusted the economy would go into a tailspin.

Suddenly I had an epiphany that made me realize why my family was nothing at all for me to worry about.

I remembered my first trip to the state fair. If you've ever been, this will work for you, too. In less than five minutes you could be saying, "You know what? We're all right. We're dang near royalty."

A state fair is the only place where you can see people who were born, raised, married, and had families without ever leaving their own property. You see people to whom you know walking upright is a fairly new idea. You see people who make you feel guilty for ever thinking you had a weight problem. You see people K Mart would ask to leave. You see people so ugly that you have to get somebody else to verify it.

"Come here, y'all gotta see this man! Get outta line, it's worth it! Over by the cotton candy. Don't look, don't look. Is that the hairiest back you've ever seen. Looks like Bigfoot in a tank top. Oh God, it's a woman! Oh, and she's got kids. Somebody slept with that woman!! Oh no, it's Aunt Betty!"

I think it's only right that if I reveal secrets about my family I have to share a few intimate details about Gregg's. After all, our daughters are the product of our genes, and to be forewarned is to be forearmed.

Gregg's mother, Jane, God bless her, is the adrenaline poster girl. No matter what, she's always got a pot of coffee brewing at her house. She drinks coffee and smokes cigarettes day and night. If Jane goes to bed at 11:00 P.M., she'll be back up at 11:35. She'll have a cup of coffee, couple of smokes, and go back to bed until one, when she'll get up and do it all again. I finally said, "Jane, has it ever occurred to you that perhaps all this caffeine may be interfering with your sleep?" Deadly serious, she said, "No, hon. Coffee has never messed up my sleep. I get up every hour or two and have a cup."

Any time that Jane stayed at our house I could sleepwalk in the middle of the night and be sure I also had a conversation with Jane. She was always down in the kitchen with her coffee and her smokes.

Her husband, Elliott, doesn't drink anymore. He probably hasn't tossed back a stiff one in over a decade. That's saying a lot. He used to own a bar in New Orleans. Elliot's got some fabulous stories. It's a city of characters and everyone who came into the bar had a name. There was the Mannequin, who always dressed impeccably. He named another guy Crime, because he never paid. He called two young women who hung out at the bar the Tar Babies, because if you ever touched them you couldn't get rid of them.

Elliot's funniest story is from the time when he used to drink. Apparently he was out one night and didn't quite make it home. The next morning about 7:00 A.M., he called Jane and said, "Jane, you gotta come get me. I don't know where my car is."

Naturally, she was awake and had already cleaned the kitchen. Jane said, "Elliott, where are you."

"I'm at the big building."

"Elliott, we live in New Orleans," she said. "There's lots of big buildings."

"You know, Jane, the *big building*." But he wasn't making any sense and Jane got pissed.

"Elliott, put down the damn phone and go ask somebody where you are!"

He set down the phone and a minute later came back. "I'm at the Gulf & Western building, Jane."

"Elliott," she said, "you're across the damn street!"

Elliot later told me he called it "the big building" because when they stood on their balcony and looked out the window, there was this big building obstructing the view.

The odd thing about my family is that we're all so different. Big Jim and Carole were married for fourteen years. Big Jim smokes, drinks, and is a womanizer; Carole doesn't smoke, doesn't drink, and goes to church five times a week. (I've always wondered what they had in common.) My brother is totally gregarious. He wants to try every food and everything in the world once. I'm that way, too. My sister prefers to stay at home.

When my folks divorced, it was probably hardest on Jennifer. She's always heard a drummer that Jay and I didn't hear. When she turned twelve, she got a phone for Christmas. We didn't really see her again until she got married. We called her bedroom "the vault" because she always locked the door. We'd play in the yard and she'd sit in her window smoking cigarettes, with the fan blowing the smoke out, talking on the phone with her friends. My mother never knew that my sister smoked cigarettes until the day she cleaned out my sister's closet and found seventeen shoe boxes full of empty cigarette packs. I still don't get it. Why did she keep the packs? And what was wrong with my mother's sense of smell?

As you know, divorce is a way of life in my family. In fact, my brother, Jay, is probably the first Foxworthy since Columbus landed to have stayed married to his first wife. This has caused us some concern. It's not that we don't love Rhonda, but we had a streak going. On more than one occasion I've called Jay and said, "Hey, I saw your wife downtown drinking with another guy yesterday."

My brother and I, and even my sister, have often said that we wouldn't be surprised if someday the doorbell rang and there stood a young woman who said, "Hi, I'm your sister."

What would surprise me is if it didn't happen at least four or five times.

Perhaps you have finally decided that all the clichés about Southern families are true. You know the ones: We all marry our sisters and look for UFOs. Well, they're not true. I'm just dating my sister and I couldn't swear it *wasn't* a weather balloon.

I think we did have some cousins marry on both sides of the family. Well, I'm *sure* on my mother's side. But they weren't first cousins because that would be sick. I think they were first cousins once removed. Most states have laws against intrafamily marriage, anyway. Unfortunately, having to pass a law to prevent something that to many seems entirely natural doesn't make us Rednecks look too good.

Once, a fan asked me to try and describe being Southern. I know he didn't mean Redneck, but the answer was still easy. I said it was a night at Stone Mountain.

Stone Mountain, just outside Atlanta, is the world's largest rock. They call it a mountain, but it's a single piece of granite. On one side there's a pasture in a clearing and every night from spring until fall it's the biggest tourist attraction in Georgia. Families gather at sundown with picnic baskets to watch the laser show on the side of the rock. They play music and the beams flash and draw pictures and the characters dance. The theme is always patriotic. The lasers will trace pine trees and make a picture of Ray Charles, and he'll sing *Georgia*. They'll also throw in *God Bless America* and *Proud to Be an American*. People just sit there with their kids and their coolers of beer and sandwiches, and stare like these were visions from heaven.

Carved into the other side of Stone Mountain are the Three Horsemen of the Confederacy. It's the world's largest carving—bigger than Mount Rushmore. During the laser show the thing goes jet-black and then the laser outlines it in perfect detail. The horses are dead still. Then Elvis starts singing *Dixie*. One of the horse's nostrils flares and he shakes his head, and the horses start walking. Soon, *Dixie* blends into *The Battle Hymn of the Republic*, and the horses start running. That's when you see the hair on the necks of grown men in cat hats and flannel shirts stand up. They drop their chicken and dissolve into sobbing messes.

"You okay, Daddy?"

"No no no, I'm not okay.

By the way, for singing the song, Elvis gets all the chicken that hits the ground.

Another great thing about Stone Mountain is the game ranch, where you can walk through and pet different animals. They stock the place with magnificent white-tailed deer; native to the East Coast, they sport huge antler racks. Every three years or so some guy can't stand it anymore and shoots one through the fence. That's real hunting. He always gets caught trying to drag it out.

"Where'd you get him?"

"He was right next to the candy dispenser. Just gave him a graham cracker and boom! I popped him."

A Redneck for sure. No "might be" about it.

If I didn't know better, I'd say he was part of my family.

Redneck or Not... Here I Come

People always ask me "How do you come up with these Redneck jokes?" By now you realize it's not like I had to do a lot of research. It's pretty much a case of "Welcome to my life."

But for those of you who *still* don't get it, I thought it would be fun (and instructive) to share some of the real stories behind a few of my favorite Redneck lines. Think of it as a peek inside Granddaddy's shed. Maybe you'll finally discover what those plastic bags of rabbits' tails are really for.

"If you know how many bales of hay your car will hold . . ."

Ten. I had a Camaro. I could put three in the trunk, six in the backseat, and one in the passenger seat. The reason I know is because Big Jim decided he could make some extra money by selling farm hay. On my days off from school he would send me to the farm to get the hay which he'd sell at two bucks a pop. For instance, the people down the road needed ten bales for their horse. Like the pizza man, I delivered. I'd drive four hours just to make twenty dollars, of which I had to spend sixteen for gas.

"If you see no need to stop at rest stops because you have an empty milk jug in the car . . ."

That's how we dealt with bathroom stops on the way to the fair. It takes too much time to pull of the highway and pee. You lose two valuable minutes and guys don't want to waste that kind of time on a road trip. You can pee in a milk jug instead. Just hope you also brought the cap with you. Even mom would do it if it was cold.

"If Thanksgiving dinner was ruined because you ran out of ketchup . . ."

Honestly, this isn't that funny to me because we have ketchup on the table during Thanksgiving dinner. We do! Sometimes people come over for dinner and observe our liberal use of ketchup and get grossed out. If there's ever a ketchup ban, my family will die. I put ketchup on everything. I used to put it on scrambled eggs. When I did it as a kid my dad would look at my plate and go, "Oh, for God's sake, looks like a damn Korean war over there." I also put ketchup on grits. And turkey. Tried it on ice cream once just because somebody said, "You'd probably put ketchup on ice cream." I'll tell you the truth, it's not that bad. Ketchup is also good with potato chips. We call it the poor man's dip. It makes a fine spaghetti sauce, too.

"If you've ever hit a bump on the highway and lost half your worldly possessions . . . "

Big Jim again. When we had the farm, Big Jim always made us load up the truck with junk from the farm and take it to the dump. Thing was, we always came back from the dump with more than we took. In the middle of throwing things away, Big Jim would say, "Oh, man, somebody threw away a good toilet down here." So stuff would be going out one side of the truck and in the other side. It was a good old Chevy truck, too. We knocked the passenger door off three different times. I'd be trying to back the truck through the woods into the dump and my brother would hold the door open, look out, and say, "Come back! Come back!" Then I'd hit a tree he wasn't watching and the door would pop right off.

After we unloaded and reloaded at the dump we took our new possessions back to the farm and put them in the place where the old junk had been. A year or so later Daddy would go, "God dang, we've gotta clean out behind the barn." Then we'd pick up that stuff and go off to the dump again for a new load.

Whenever we did this we weren't really big on the tie-down theory. We'd just throw the junk in the truck bed and take off. So many times cruising down I-285, the interstate in Atlanta, we'd have to pull over to the side of the road so Big Jim and I could run out to the center lane to pick up a sofa that had bounced off the back of the truck. It was embarrassing to a fourteen-year-old. Cars sped by at eighty miles an hour and we were out there trying to pull a sofa off the highway. The sofa wouldn't even be worth twenty bucks, yet we risked life and limb to save it.

Once my friend Steve and I were hauling two mattresses and box springs we'd gotten at Goodwill back to Big Jim's farm to use on the homemade bunk beds at the farm. At some point during the drive he threw a cigarette out the window. I turned to Steve and I said, "That didn't go in the back of the truck, did it?"

"No, no."

About five miles later I looked in the rearview mirror and saw the back of the truck engulfed in flames. I pulled off the road, jumped in the truck bed, and started hauling the mattress onto the shoulder. My first thought was to pee on them, but if you've ever tried to put out a mattress fire then you know it's damn near impossible. Mattresses are like the trick birthday candles that you can never blow out. So Steve got the cooler out of the cab and began pouring perfectly good cold beer over the fire. I said, "That's good beer, man! Don't be wasting our good beer."

When we showed up at Big Jim's we had one box spring and half a mattress. He wasn't real happy about that. It was an investment of eleven dollars down the drain.

"If you've ever shot rats at the dump for entertainment . . ."

My granddaddy used to take a magnetic flashlight, stick it to the side of a .22 rifle, and shoot rats at the dump at night. It's great and cheap entertainment since .22 shells are probably two cents apiece. That's a hundred shots for two bucks.

If you hit them just right they usually roll. Sometimes when the flashlight beam hits them they'll just sit still and you can pick them off easy. But that isn't really a sport, so it's best to have a friend holler at the rat while you're aiming.

"If you refused to watch the Academy Awards when Smokey and the Bandit was snubbed for Best Picture . . ."

The last time Big Jim went to the movies was to see *Smokey and the Bandit*. I think he felt like it would never get any better than that. It had it all: a cute woman, car wrecks, fights. You don't need anything else. Plus, he loved Jackie Gleason. My dad could quote his lines. In fact, he'll still walk into an old Hickory House restaurant and go, "Gimme a diablo sandwich and a large Dr. Pepper, and make it snappy 'cause I'm in a damn hurry." Thanks, Dad.

"If you've ever stolen a bulldozer . . ."

One of my stepbrother's friends stole a bulldozer and got pulled over while driving down I-75 in Atlanta. I know what you're thinking. I don't know where he was headed, but he wasn't getting there very fast. It's hard to blend into traffic. I don't care if you tuck in behind a van, it's hard to look nonchalant when you're sitting in a bulldozer on the interstate.

"If you've ever been too drunk to fish . . ."

That was me. When I worked at Kroger a couple of coworkers and I drove all night one time to go fishing. It didn't dawn on us that perhaps we might need sleep. Or that we shouldn't drink. When we got there in the morning we didn't even have hangovers; we were still so drunk. But how drunk do you have to be not to fish? I kept having little blackouts—two or three seconds max—and I dropped my hundred dollar rod and reel straight to the bottom of the lake. Those things don't float.

"If 'Foxy Lady' is airbrushed on the front license plate of your car . . ."

Saw it in Panama City, Florida. Swear to God.

"If you've ever driven a Camaro into the top of a tree . . ."

This happened down near where my uncle lives at Lake Jodico. Somebody got drunk, drove off the road, and the car got airborne and landed in the tree next to the house. You know and I know that somebody took his friends back down there to see it, too.

"Come here, you ain't gonna believe this shit."

"If the Salvation Army ever declines your mattress . . ."

When Gregg and I got together she did something that all women do when they're getting ready to move in with a man. They go through your stuff and see if anything you own is anything they want in the new place. Don't count on it. Nothing that the guy has is ever going to make it onto the permanent list. You've got to fight like hell for just one or two items.

"Well, you know, I really like that table."

"Okay, we'll use my dresser and we'll use my bed. And, oh God, what is *this*? I can't imagine." I ended up taking a bunch of stuff to the Salvation Army, including my mattress. When we took it off the truck they took one look at it and said, "No. No thank you." They were right. Lord knows who all had slept on it. It had so many stains on it. It was really nasty.

It really makes you feel good about yourself when homeless people cannot use the stuff that you've been living on.

"If your dad walks you to school because you're both in the same grade . . ."

This was inspired by a guy who was in the fourth grade with me. His name was Eddie. The rest of us weighed fifty pounds, he drove a car. He used to mesmerize us in the bathroom by showing us his pubic hair.

"If you've ever brought a siphon hose to show and tell . . ."

Big Jim taught me to siphon gas out of a truck when I was still in elementary school. You always end up with a bad taste in your mouth. If there's some other way to do it, please tell me. One time Burns siphoned too much gas and got a mouthful. He spit it all out, but he burped the rest of the weekend and smelled like an Amoco station. On the positive side, there probably weren't many kids in the fifth grade who knew how to do that.

"If the flood history of your area can be seen on the living room walls . . ."

I was watching CNN when I heard these people who lived on a flood plain talking about how they had been wiped out in a flood—but it wasn't as bad as how they'd been wiped out the year before. And the way they were wiped out two years before was *really* bad. That's when I yelled at the TV: "Here's an idea: Why don't you move?!"

"If you've ever shot a deer from inside your house . . ."

Ask my Uncle William. It was the best deer he ever got. William shot him from the bathroom window, and I'm pretty sure Uncle William was somehow indisposed at the time. Of course, now he tells it as like, "I shot it right out behind the house." Well, the *deer* was out behind the house.

The truth is that he was sitting in the bathroom reading the latest issue of *Hound Dog Weekly* when he spotted the deer through the window. So without pulling his pants up, he did a little duckwalk to the gun rack, grabbed his loaded 30–30, came back, cracked the window, and shot the deer. I'm assuming he cleaned up before he went out to gut it.

We found this out because Aunt Rose told on him. Apparently the reverb of the gunshot echoing off the shower tiles scared the crap out of everyone in the house. Dishes broke.

"If you've ever financed your tattoo . . ."

When I worked a job in Lexington, Kentucky, I saw a tattoo parlor with a sign painted on the window: "Financing Available." My first thought was "How do you repossess one of these when somebody doesn't pay?" Meanwhile, somewhere a guy is pointing to his arm, saying, "Three more payments, this sumbitch is *mine*."

"If the receptionist is responsible for checking the rat traps at your place of business . . ."

I was scheduled to do an early-morning radio show in Oklahoma. When I got there at 6:30 A.M. I had to wait in the lobby for someone to let me in. Just to kill the time I looked under the credenza, and there was a rat trap with a dead rat under the bar. When someone finally showed up, I said, "You've got a dead rat under

there.'' The woman said, deadly serious, "That's the receptionist's job. She checks them every day." She just left it there. When
I finished the interview, I stopped in the lobby and asked the receptionist if she'd gotten the rat. She said, "Yeah. He was a nice
one!''

"Stacey? Could you check the rat traps and get me a cup of
coffee?''

"If you've ever peed in an ice machine . . ."
When the gang stops at a gas station and everyone has to relieve
himself, it's hard to find places to go. Usually, one guy is already
peeing in the toilet, another is peeing in the sink, and if you've
gotta go, man, you've gotta go. And peeing in the ice machine by
the gas station office is creative. Most Rednecks will risk going to
jail if it means they can get their buddies to laugh. This is even
funnier if you are a woman.

"If you run down the bowling alley and slide into the pins . . ."
There's actually a competition like that every year in Illinois.
These guys wear silk shirts, get a running start, and the idea is to
hit the pins with their bodies. To get a strike they have to turn
sideways as they collide with the pins. Afterward, most of the con-
testants have huge blue welts on their foreheads where they hit the
pins wrong trying to pick up a spare. No one wears helmets. This
is one of those things you see on television and think, "Thank
you, God. There but for fortune go I."

Could be worse, though. As I mentioned earlier, just after Gregg
and I moved to Los Angeles, I spotted an ad in the newspaper for
a national farting contest. If you're a comedian, that's an attention
grabber right there. My first thought was that it had to be a bunch
of fraternity guys. Then I read the list of who would compete:
"Three-Time Nebraska Champion, Bill 'Bo-Bo' Browner." I told
Gregg I had to go. I had too many questions. Were these guys like
other entertainers. Did they have groupies? Were women hanging

around backstage going, ''When we first started coming to see you, we wouldn't even gag or anything. But now, you make my brother vomit.''

''Oh thank you, little lady.''

Would I see fat guys eating beans right out of the can?

''Please, no lighted cigarettes in the auditorium.''

One of the few regrets I have in life is not finding a way to attend this contest.

"If your hobby is stealing road signs ..."

I stole many. There's an art to it. They're not just wood. They've got bolts. To do the job correctly, you've got to carry the right size wrench and a big screwdriver. You hold the bolt on one side and crank it on the other. But you've got to do it at night. You drop one guy off and then you drive away, and you let the guy work. If you're the job man, you shinny up a pole and you crank. If a car comes by you drop down and lie flat on the side of the road, and wait until the car goes away. It can take a long time. On a busy street you may only get one or two wrench turns at a time. On a country road it's a better deal. The hardest to swipe are interstate signs. One thing to remember, you don't steal road signs just for the sake of stealing. It has to be something you want. for instance, if you find a sign that says ''DANGEROUS CURVES AHEAD'' and the pictured curve in any way resembles a breast, it will be something you need. Dex got us one of those.

One time Buddy Hammond and I decided to steal the road sign with our street name on it. We weren't really good thieves because we were stealing it at four o'clock in the afternoon. I sat on Buddy's shoulders and worked the bolt while cars kept driving by. As we were leaving, Buddy thought he saw a cop car cruise by, so after we had the sign in the house for a few minutes, we went back and put the sign up again. It was a lot more difficult than taking it down.

I don't list this on my résumé, but for a year or two, while going down to the farm, I may have ranked in the top five nationally in the sport of hitting road signs with beer bottles at high speeds. I was great at it. I could hit them with anything. I got so good I could hit mile-marker signs with a pony Miller bottle, without even leaning out of the car. People always want to throw the bottle *at* the sign. That's wrong. The trick is to gauge how fast the car is going, and then you throw it straight out. All you want to do is get height and distance from the car.

When you hit a sign, the glass shatters on the grass just off the shoulder. Don't feel too bad about that because if you've got to pull over, you've probably got a flat tire anyway. So what's the big deal?

Eventually hitting the signs got boring. Buddy Hammond was pretty damn good at driving and throwing one over the top of the car and hitting a road sign. I got bored hitting signs on my side of the road, as well. So I'd sit on the passenger window sill while we were going seventy and throw them over the top of the car, across the other lane, and hit signs on the other side of the road. What could possibly go wrong? All I had to do was sneeze and I would have been dead.

Never got caught at that, either.

"If you've ever painted your car with house paint . . ."
Danny Chastain had an old station wagon that he called the Eggmobile. It looked like pure crap so one day we decided to paint it. We weren't kids with a lot of money, so we went to the drugstore and bought spray paint. We figured we'd spray it black in Burns' side yard. About halfway through the job, the wind started blowing. It was fall and soon leaves were stuck all over the body. Every time we pulled a leaf off, it left a pockmark, and soon the car went from being the Eggmobile to being the Acnemobile.

"If the primary color of your car is Bondo . . ."
That was my Datsun 280-Z. I had to have the car because it was

so fast. In fact, that car inspired several Redneck lines. Another was *"If you have to get a tetanus shot to drive your car . . ."* The car was originally from Michigan and it was so rusted that you could pretty much put your foot through it. Another was *"If your car uses more oil than gas . . ."* This car burned oil but also burned rubber going into fourth gear.

Anyway, as I got money, I had the body redone. It was Bondo color for a year before I finally got it all painted.

"If your dog can smoke cigarettes . . ."

Somebody who worked with my dad at IBM had a basset hound named Boozer who would drink beer out of his bowl. Then he would sit there with a cigarette in his mouth.

The Redneck Aptitude Test

You've learned how Redneck jokes are created. Now let's see what you remember. Give yourself a point for each right answer. On second thought, just give yourself a point for trying to answer. No use making this too difficult. High score gets a lifetime supply of Doe-in-Heat.

Part One: Just Pick One

1. What does a divorcée call herself?
   a. Lonely
   b. In recovery
   c. Hot to Trot

2. What's the best way to move the wedding party from the church to the reception?
   a. Car pool
   b. Limousines
   c. Announce there's a keg at the reception

3. What should I say to the bride in the receiving line?
   a. Congratulations
   b. Enjoyed the ceremony
   c. I like your mustache (and your baby is real cute)

4. At what point should a host ask a guest to leave?
   a. After coffee
   b. When you go to bed
   c. When you go to work

5. It is all right to make an off-color toast at:
   a. A family reunion
   b. A wedding
   c. A funeral

6. Does proper etiquette allow a woman to wear shorts in the city?
   a. Yes, if it matches her tube top
   b. Yes, but both legs should be cut the same length
   c. Who goes to the city?

7. What should you do if you can't remember someone's name?
   a. Ignore them
   b. Call him Hoss
   c. Pretend to be blind
   d. Look at his belt buckle

8. What should you do when the national anthem is played?
   a. Stand up
   b. Take off your John Deere hat
   c. Turn off the TV and go to bed
   d. Put down your beer

9. If the person next to you on the airplane is a chatterbox, you should . . .
   a. Pretend you're asleep

b. Tell them you're a Jehovah's Witness

c. Pass gas

10. Why should one check suitcases and other items instead of taking them on planes?

    a. It's rude to other passengers who need the leg room your cooler takes

    b. Crowded aisles are a hassle for flight attendants

    c. It's hard to put a goat in the overhead compartment

11. When you desire service at your table, you should . . .

    a. Whistle

    b. Beat your beer bottle on the ashtray

    c. Throw a biscuit at the waiter

12. How should one introduce a speaker?

    a. Stand up and check your fly

    b. Beat your beer bottle with a spoon

    c. Holler "Y'all shut up. We got somebody that wants to talk!"

    d. All of the above, in that order

13. How do you write a proper letter of resignation?

    a. "Adios, butt-heads"

    b. Spit on the desk and work it around with your finger

    c. Dear Sirs: I love the bowling business but can no longer handle the pressures of league night

14. If a bug crawls out of your lettuce while dining at a friend's house you . . .

    a. Scream

    b. Eat it discreetly, using your salad fork

    c. Mask it with your coffee cup

    d: Pocket it for a future fishing trip

15. If you encounter a fish bone, you should . . .

    a. Spit it into your napkin

    b. Save it to pick your teeth with later

    c. Open your mouth, stick out your tongue and announce, "Look, see-food"

16. How do you use chopsticks?

    a. Ask the waiter

    b. Sharpen them with your knife and stab food

    c. I don't know, and it don't matter if you're from the South

17. When looking for a new home, the prime considerations are . . .

    a. Convenience of schools and shopping

    b. Property values in the community

    c. Whether or not your old lady can swing the payments on her Dunkin' Donuts salary

18. A Redneck should not name his son Theodore because . . .

    a. No stock car drivers are named Theodore

    b. It's too long to write on a shirt pocket

    c. It would require a huge bladder to write his name in the snow

19. When disposing of beer cans while fishing, you should . . .

    a. Use a handy recycling bag

    b. Crush them against your forehead and skim them across the surface

    c. Fill them with water so they sink to the bottom

20. How far is too far on a first date?

    a. Halfway

    b. All the way

    c. Chattanooga

Part Two: Roadkill and Other Edibles

If you have more than five of these in your icebox . . . you've got a serious problem.

1. Piña colada mix
2. Dip
3. One shelf devoted to beer
4. Leftover SPAM
5. Rotten watermelon, with seeds
6. Frozen burritos, thawed more than a week
7. Cool Whip
8. Pigs' feet or tongue
9. Pot of macaroni (including spoon—bonus points)
10. Open can of dog food (No tinfoil cover—bonus points)
11. Cigarettes (by the carton—bonus points)
12. Suppositories in the butter dish
13. Collection of Taco Bell taco sauce packets
14. Half a burger (more than five days old—bonus points)
15. Spilled Kool-Aid
16. Yoo-Hoos
17. Batteries
18. Deviled ham
19. Half a Big Gulp
20. Deer sausage
21. Used cooking grease
23. Empty pizza box
24. Pickled eggs
25. Baking soda (extra boxes—one bonus point each)

Part Three: Redneck Cinema

Which of these classic Redneck movies have you seen?
1. Smokey and the Bandit
2. Walking Tall
3. Deliverance
4. Gator
5. Cannonball Run I and II
6. White Lightning

7. The Longest Yard
8. Ernest (any)
9. Mad Max
10. Halloween
11. Katie: Portrait of a Centerfold
12. Jan Michael Vincent film (any)

Part Four: The Rube Tube

If you haven't watched more than three of these shows, you are definitely not Redneck material.
1. Any fishing show
2. The Andy Griffith Show
3. The Beverly Hillbillies
4. Green Acres
5. Mr. Ed
6. Adam 12
7. F-Troop
8. Mutual of Omaha's Wild Kingdom
9. WWF (rasslin')
10. The People's Court
11. Cops (to help locate your relatives)
12. Charlie's Angels
13. Club Dance
14. Brewster McCloud
15. Baywatch

Part Five: Redneck Wear

How many of these items are in your wardrobe, good buddy?
1. Any convenience store cap
2. Jeans with hems walked off
3. Orange vest
4. Camouflage underwear

5. Snakeskin boots
6. Hulk-a-Mania T-shirt
7. Acid-washed tuxedo
8. A Harley vest
9. Shirts without sleeves
10. Sleeves without shirts
11. Shirt with race-car picture
12. Tie-dyed nightgown
13. Jaclyn Smith negligee
14. Panties big enough to slow a dragster
15. Hank Williams Junior sweatshirt

Part Six: Redneck Home and Garden

A true Redneck will have ten or more of these in his front yard.

1. A major appliance
2. A motor hanging from a tree
3. An oil pan still full
4. A pair of men's underwear
5. Chickens (live)
6. Half a motorcycle
7. More than twelve tires
8. A deer carcass
9. Corrugated metal
10. A car door
11. Coffee can flower pots
12. A buried pet
13. Crime scene tape
14. Pile of gravel
15. Fish skulls (not alive)
16. Dogs on chains
17. Past-due bills
18. One hunting boot
19. The front door

20. TV dinner trays
21. Pink plastic flamingos with the heads shot off

Part Seven: Redneck Decor

These items are on my walls. What about yours?

1. Deer head (extra points if deer wears sunglasses, cap, or beads)
2. Beer mirrors
3. Dried food
4. Velvet painting of Elvis
5. License plates
6. Poster of Dale Earnhart
7. Picture of your wife on the toilet
8. Fish (any variety)
9. Gun rack
10. Flags
11. Motley Crüe poster
12. Hooters calendar
13. Autographed picture of Rick Flair
14. Spit

How'd you do? Don't worry if you didn't pass. You can keep repeating the second grade until you get it right *and* you and your kid can walk to school together. As for the rest of you, now you know why I say that being Redneck does not depend on where you reside. It's more a glorious absence of sophistication. Whether temporary or permanent, Redneck is simply a state of mind where some people live and others just come for a long visit. I think there's a little bit of Redneck in us all.

Now pass the pickled eggs and deer sausage. I've got *Smokey and the Bandit* on the VCR, my CAT cap on my head, a six-pack in the cooler, and I'm settling in for the afternoon.

The Road to Stardom Ain't Necessarily Paved

It's easy for a Redneck to become famous among his own. Just hit a highway sign with a beer can out a car window at fifty miles an hour. Have a favorite T-shirt declared offensive in thirteen states. Shoot a deer from inside your home. Know the most ways to sneak liquor into high school sporting events. Eat a double-bacon cheeseburger in one bite. Send a photocopy of your bare butt along with your Christmas cards.

Do any one and they'll tell your story at deer hunts, dove shoots, and keggers clear to the county line.

But sometimes a Redneck becomes well known by people beyond family, friends, creditors, and the local law enforcement community. When this happens, he must quickly learn that widespread recognition involves greater rewards, larger responsibilities, and the possibility of being arrested by mistake. Sometimes the price of stardom for these special few is simply learning to write. Scratching an "X" just won't cut it when fans ask for an autograph. In any case, life will never again be as simple as just having to quickly reassemble a transmission in the bathtub before company arrives.

It would be nice if there were a manual explaining how to be a celebrity. Unfortunately, it's pretty much a learn-as-you-go proposition.

One evening when I was washing dishes and watching the TV, I realized that I might be more well known than even I suspected. I saw a commercial for an ABC show called *Before They Were Stars*. Suddenly there I was on-screen, in 1985, doing stand-up on amateur night in Ufalla, Alabama. My shirt was pretty cool but never in my wildest dreams did I imagine that that old videotape would ever air on national television. It really stopped me in mid-scrub. I said to my wife, "Honey, if I'm on a before-they-were-stars show, does this mean I'm a star now?"

She handed me the crusty roast pan; a reality check if ever there was one. We both knew that even after more than ten years of entertaining everyone from coeds on spring break to the chief executive at the Ford Theater, that I still didn't think of myself as any more than just a regular guy. Of course, once I could run out for milk and diapers without a second thought, but now, people I didn't even know—including some fifth and sixth cousins who, I should point out, have *just recently* declared themselves family relations—think of me as some sort of celebrity.

I still don't believe it. The company that books my concerts always tells me I have the smallest backstage catering bill in the history of entertainment. At one of my biggest shows last year, we had three six-packs of Sprites and 7-Ups—in case somebody came up—a pot of coffee, some candy bars, and a container of Tic-Tacs. The tab came to almost $25.

As you can tell, none of this has gone to my head.

A person's idea of celebrity constantly changes. When I was twelve years old, just seeing the sportscaster from WSB, Channel Two in Atlanta, in a restaurant, prevented me from eating because I was so excited. All I could do was whisper, ''Art Eckman's right over there!'' I never talked to him, of course, because you didn't approach Art Eckman in *public*. Nooo.

Now I see Art Eckman on ESPN doing ''Motor World'' and I still get excited. I just don't understand why my wife thinks it's strange when I point at the TV and whisper at the top of my lungs, ''Art Eckman's right over there!''

Any entertainer can perform for years without crossing the line where one day he notices that people notice him more than he notices them. Then it happens. At first, the lingering stares can feel awkward. You're not sure why people gawk at you so intently. Suddenly you're wondering if your shirt is on inside out. If your socks match. Are your pants pulled up all the way? Are you even wearing pants? The thought of dandruff is scary because the flakes would have to be the size of tadpoles for someone to see them at that distance. If it's none of the above, that's when the thought that maybe someone recognizes you might creep into your head.

Just hope it's not your parole officer.

I have performed across this country more times than most of my childhood friends have learned to count, and even I have suffered from the delusion that everyone knows who I am. Fortunately, that's just when I am forced to confront my own foolishness. Just because I say, ''Hi, I'm Jeff Foxworthy,'' not everyone will go, ''Ohhh!'' Lots of times, no one does. They have no idea who I am. This is toughest when I've stepped outside the concert hall for some air before the show and the stage door locks behind me. When the guy taking tickets at the front door doesn't know me from Spike, it has a way of planting one's feet back on the ground. Suddenly you're scrubbing the roast pan.

Being or not being recognized is both better than *kind of* not being recognized. It cracks me up when someone asks, ''Are you somebody?''

''I hope so,'' I usually reply.

''Who are you?''

''Well, if you don't know it doesn't matter, right?''

Well, not always. Not everyone who stares at a celebrity is a fan. Once, while walking through the Detroit airport, a group of men suddenly locked their eyes on me. ''Okay,'' I thought, ''I can take a compliment. I just hope they don't ask for autographs in awkward places.'' I smiled politely and kept walking. They didn't smile back. Suddenly one of the men yelled, ''Hey! Who are you? What's your name?'' I walked faster.

It was freezing cold, I wanted to get to my hotel, and I was in no mood for meeting people who didn't even seem to know me. As I walked, I asked myself if I'd made any jokes onstage the night before that I might regret today. Had I said *anything* at all that would cause ten men in dull business suits to follow me from one city to another?

That's when they surrounded me. One guy said, ''Let's see some ID.'' I said, ''Who wants to know?'' I figured out they were cops when the guy flashed his badge. I'm sharp that way. My wallet and airline ticket were in my coat pocket. I reached in to get them. They pulled their guns on me. I'm not lying. I've seen this happen so many times in the movies you'd think I'd know better.

I eased my hand back.

Later, they apologized for the inconvenience and told me they were searching for a guy on the Ten Most Wanted List who looked an awful lot like me. Same height, weight, and coloring. Only, it seemed, not nearly as nice. Mr. Most Wanted would not have wiped his feet before getting into the squad car.

"The guy kidnaped and murdered five people," one cop said. Then they let me go and gave me some advice: "Be careful. This might happen again."

It didn't, but a couple of weeks later, a buddy of mine in Baltimore sent me something he'd discovered in his local post office: a Wanted Poster.

"Fox, you're not gonna believe this," he wrote. "Look how much this guy looks like you!" He was right. Same mustache, same haircut . . . we could have been twins. I don't know if the Detroit police ever caught up with this man. I hope so. But the memory of being drawn down on still lingers. That's why now, when strangers approach, my smile usually says, "Howdy," but my eyes say, "I swear I didn't do it."

I wonder if my wife would ever buy this explanation?

There are many degrees of celebrity. For instance, there's fame and then there's *fame*. When I was a teenager playing air-guitar in front of the mirror, I imagined that being famous involved many women and a lot more leisure time. Now I think fame is like money. Any time you get to where you think you've got it, you don't have to look very far to see somebody who's got a lot more than you.

One type of fame is called "Only *You* Think You're a Celebrity." This is not the real thing, but a delusional state that is often incurable. Even with years of therapy it's hard to convince some people that others don't know who the hell they are. In clinical terms this is known as the "Rumor in your own time, legend in your own room" syndrome.

There is also "Fifteen-Minute" fame. If you ever get that far, the trick is to make it stick. Good examples are any panelists on a daytime talk show, or Kato Kaelin. He's already had about seventeen minutes. His time is really up. He'd better check the buzzer. Now if I could only get him to vacate the guest house.

More types include notorious phenomenons, personalities, stars, superstars, legends, and the kind of ultimate celebrity that both you and I don't really ever want to be. The last is easy to spot: You know you've reached that pinnacle when *someone else* can make a living being your celebrity double.

Once you become like Elvis or Michael Jackson, that's not celebrity. That's prison. Too bad neither one has helped his own cause much. Elvis used to bitch he couldn't go to the movie theater, but maybe if he didn't take twelve cars and wear the cape, he could've snuck in and seen the show.

I finally understood the enormity of Elvis—and I'm just talking about his fame—once I toured Graceland. I'll never forget the moment I stood in the Jungle Room and surveyed the green shag carpet and the leopard skin throne. I had one all-consuming thought: "You cannot give Rednecks money. You can't! We don't know what to do with it." Somebody should have had the guts to go, "E, man, this is really tacky stuff here. Perhaps a nice Ethan Allan sectional would be better."

Elvis also had a whole hallway—more like a runway—lined with gold and platinum records. That's a problem I *do* understand. Now, all of a sudden, *I've* got gold and platinum records. What I need is a sensible outdoor storage shed to put them in. I've also got pictures of myself with guys like Johnny Carson, David Letterman, Bob Hope. Gregg likes the new double-platinum albums because they've got mahogany frames, and she wants to put them up in the living room. I can't. They'd detract from the antlers and my collection of cologne bottles shaped like automobiles.

My big question is: At what point does my ego allow me to put up this stuff in my own home? I'm uncomfortable. It's like a salute to myself. I think I should just put these mementos in my office where people can walk in and see them if they move a couple of packing crates and look around really hard.

There is one picture, though, that I *did* want to put up. I once worked at a comedy club in Daytona Beach during spring break. They took my publicity photo, which was really nice, blew it up, and made a sign that read, "Back by popular demand! Jeff Foxworthy." Right. I'm *sure* those college kids demanded that I come back. They probably thought I was the Budweiser delivery man. But the photo was cool and my wife framed it. Now it's in my office, and I can honestly say it looks really stupid next to me with Johnny Carson, me with Milton Berle, and me with Travis Tritt. "Oh, and there's Jeff, back by popular demand at the CocoHut in Daytona Beach."

Some celebrities don't know how to act when a fan wants an autograph. I think "gracious" is a good word to keep in mind. Signing anything from slightly used table napkins to sweaty chests is easy and just being polite. I'm happy to oblige. I remember when no one wanted my signature except on speeding tickets. If I could, I'd also give away twenty-dollar bills with each autograph, just to show my appreciation for your support. (If you believe that, please place this book next to your copy of *UFO's Are Real!* Not a bad read, by the way.)

What if a fan wants more than an autograph? That can be confusing. I've sat in a hotel lobby, and all of a sudden somebody just slaps the hell out of my back and goes, "Hey, next time yer in town, come out to the house and have dinner with us. You come in a day early, by God, and we'll go huntin'. I'll put you on some squirrels." Honestly, I'd like to. Maybe next year.

Otherwise, I have no problem with being recognized: on the

street, in the supermarket, or even at the Victoria's Secret store over in the mall. Hey, it's tough, waiting thirty days between catalogs. A man's got to keep up with fashion.

Here's something I learned: When you meet a celebrity you admire you should say, "Hello" and "It's a thrill to meet you." Then shake their hand and leave. The longer you stay the less you're welcome—unless they *want* to keep talking. Just don't mistake the smile and automatic head nod as a signal that you should run down your life story. Celebrities appreciate your good wishes. They like to know that something they do is all that makes your life worth living. They're probably even thrilled to hear about how their sitcom/movie/album, etc. made the week you spent in the hospital, for double hernia surgery, bearable. But please don't feel obligated to describe the recuperation process, especially if it involves drainage, rot, or highly infectious liquids.

Am I rude to say all this? It's just good fan manners. I'll give you another great tip: Don't bug famous people while they're eating. Whenever my mother is in L.A., she wants to go to Dan Tana's restaurant. She thinks it's the best Italian place in the world, which means she likes it better than the Shakey's Pizza in Stockbridge, Georgia. Last time we were at Dan Tana's Bob Newhart came in with Dick Martin and sat two tables away. My mother squeezed my leg, and said, "That's Bob. That's Bob Newhart. Go over there and introduce yourself to Bob."

I said, "Mother, they're eating. I will *never* go interrupt somebody's meal just to say hello."

Well, the whole meal she wouldn't let up. "*He's* a comedian, *you're* a comedian. Go and say hello." Made sense to her.

We finally finished our meal and paid the bill. I looked over at Newhart. He'd also paid the check and was having coffee. My mother squeezed me again. "Go on!"

Against my better judgment, I said, "Okay!" I walked over to the table, head down, tail between my legs, and said, "First of all, I want to apologize so much for coming over to your table and . . ." That's when Bob Newhart looked up and said, "Jeff Foxworthy!"

"Right. And this is my mother, Carole."

He was as generous and as nice as he could be. My mother, well, you could have struck her dead with lightning. She could finally go out the door.

Some people try to meet performers after a show. Don't. If you can get a backstage pass, meet them *before* the show. I do a two-hour set and I'm pretty sweaty at the end. That's why I always feel bad when people come back for meet-and-greets and I have to put my arm around them for the picture. I smell like a buck in rut. I just stand there the whole time going, "I'm so sorry. I'm so sorry. I hope the stains come out."

I also have my heroes. When I was growing up, my heroes tended to be ballplayers. To this day one of the highlights of my life was meeting Dale Murphy. He played center field for the Braves until he ended up going to right. Won the MVP back-to-back years. He was a great player on a bunch of really bad ball clubs. But he always treated people nicely. He always signed autographs. Had a ton of class. He felt and lived up to the obligations of being a role model. I never heard anybody say anything bad about Dale Murphy, and this was a guy making $2 million a year.

One day I picked up a newspaper in the Atlanta airport. On the airplane I opened to the sports page. The headline read: "Dale Murphy Traded." I'm not ashamed to tell you that, even as a grown man of 32, on a crowded flight, tears were streaming down my face.

When you're famous, you *always* meet people who think you're their best friend. But occasionally you run into someone who actually knows you. Only you've forgotten his name. This can be a problem, unless you're from the South.

"Jeff! How the hell are ya?"

All you have to say is, "Hey, Buddy." Then you try to get some information to help you place them. "You still workin' at the same place?"

"Uh-huh."

"So where you living now?"

"Same house."

"Still married."

"Hell . . . yes."

Meanwhile, you still don't know who you're talking to.

"Well, good seein' ya'll."

"Back at ya."

Things could be worse. Once, a guy who spent three minutes with me in a comedy club bathroom ran into me eight years later and expected me to recall the whole experience as if it had happened the day before.

"You remember when we were together at the Chuckle Hut?"

I wouldn't exactly call it "together" either.

Then there was the good ole gal who cornered me at a baseball game. She couldn't stop venting about her "Yankee husband" and his side of the family. "They're such complete idiots that I'd like to choke them and drop them in the swimming pool."

Now, *that* made me want to grab the first guy who passed by and say, "Hey, Buddy? About that time we spent together at the Chuckle Hut . . ."

My fans don't send normal gifts. I already told you about the Redneck china cabinet. Rod Stewart gets a gift basket with a bottle of Dom Perignon and caviar. I get baskets with six-packs of Red

Dog, some chewing tobacco, and some grits. I bet people laugh when they send this stuff. I've now got cabinets full of grits and chewing tobacco. Look, if you must send a gift, a six-pack of Sprite, a couple of candy bars, and a cheap lease on a storehouse for all the grits and tobacco would be just fine.

Flowers can also be troublesome. Sometimes fans bring me bouquets, which is nice, but please, not in the middle of a show. Women get really upset if I don't come down to the front of the stage, pick up the flowers, and acknowledge them. (Not that they aren't appreciated by my wife when I act like I bought them for her.) Also, unlike panties, flowers are not easy to pick up with the microphone. And when I'm setting up for a punch line, it's not time to be putting anything in a vase.

I confess: I have occasionally used my celebrity to get things I wanted. I'm not talking about being able to get a table at a high-class restaurant—without a reservation. More like getting my car repaired. You see, I own a lemon. This car breaks down more than little Ricky Schroeder in the movie *The Champ*. I have even had dreams of it being stolen. I'm not a yelling guy or a throwing-things guy, but I was so pissed off at the damn thing never working that all of a sudden I found myself saying to the service manager, "You know, this car's been in here eight times, and if we don't get it fixed now I think I'm just gonna have to write a bit about it and go on the *Tonight Show* and tell everybody in America and the free world what a piece-of-crap car you guys make." Meanwhile, I could hear myself thinking, "What kind of threat is this? Listen to yourself, you dumbass."

It got fixed, though. Thank God. I didn't want to write the bit.

By far the best use of celebrity status is on airplanes. You can get that first-class seat on the upgrade, no matter who is waiting in line. They'll do it for you in a second. You walk up to the counter, lay down your boarding pass, and go, "Are there any more seats available in first class."

The person behind the counter will say, "Well, there's a long waiting list and . . ."

Then they take a look at you.

"Ohhh, yeah, I believe we *do* have one more seat up front."

I've always been proud to be one of the common people, but when I started flying in first class . . . well, anybody who thinks that all men are created equal has never flown in the front of the plane. It only took me about 2 million miles to realize that I *did* want to escape from coach class. Now when sitting in that big, comfortable, leather seat, wondering if it's okay to take home my personal salt and pepper shakers from dinner, I have the over-whelming urge to jump out of my seat, rip open the curtain, poke my head into the netherworld of coach seating, and laugh and shout, "They're puttin on the steaks now! And we're having ice cream sundaes for dessert. Ha. Ha. Ha!"

The best part of flying first class is that it's all free. "Sir, would you like another complimentary cocktail? Free headsets, any-one?" Well, some of it is free. Actually, it *should* be free consider-ing that the difference in price between a coach ticket and a first-class fare is greater than the gross national product of most third world nations. We get the leg room and the butt room, and it only costs $1,200 more. Bet you thought celebrities didn't pay a price for being able to afford the ultimate in luxury. Of course we do. I just can't figure out if we pay because we're famous or we're famous because we can pay.

If you're famous, people laugh louder at your jokes. Travis Tritt once told me, "It's funny: You get your own tour bus and people laugh a little harder at everything you say."

It's not necessarily fair. People also tend to think you're smarter. Somehow your IQ goes up. They figure that if you were smart enough to figure out how to get a job entertaining them, then you must have something on the ball. Some do, but let me tell you: A lot of idiots get famous. But only an idiot would name names.

One thing I don't do is spend any time thinking that I want to be *more* famous. In fact, being famous *every other day* would be just fine. I could show *Entertainment Tonight* my home on one day, and the next I could go out without washing my hair.

Of course, when I run out unwashed and wearing my crappy clothes, I'm sure to run into somebody with whom I went to high school. Suddenly there's the girl I had a crush on in tenth grade, who would never speak to me. She recognizes me. I can see it in the way her eyes light up that she has lived *every day* of the past fifteen years believing that she made a big mistake ignoring me and dating the varsity quarterback instead. Since graduation he's fathered her children, consumed a minibrewery's worth of bad beer, and never made it out of the shoe department at Wal-Mart. Meanwhile, she's followed my career and kept scrapbooks. I open my mouth to speak. Then she takes a good look at my raggedy sweatpants and the Braves T-shirt that's three sizes too small, and she thinks, "Maybe I did the right thing marrying Kyle."

I don't think this alternate-day celebrity plan is such a good idea after all.

My sister, Jennifer, doesn't think of me as a celebrity. But she likes the fact that other people do because through me she can meet famous people. She went to the Country Music Awards and she thought it was bizarre that her big brother Jeff would be there. That is, until Alan Jackson walked up. Then it was okay because I could say, "Alan, this is my sister."

One of the weirdest things about being famous is that I now have relatives I didn't have just a couple of years ago. But amazingly, they never call my brother or my sister or my mom. They just call me. I don't want to embarrass them here by telling you their names. (Though you'd think that after having the nerve to call me they could stand a little shame.) Let's just say they're cousins so far removed that they might as well live on the other side of the international date line. They've read that I'm now making money, so they call and say, "We jus' wan' keep the family together." I nodded in agreement and said, "What's your name again?"

I remember one conversation with a lovely woman:

"Well, it's so nice to see you're doing so well, Jeff. Things hadden been quite so good for us since Harlan hurt his back. Mama's been in and out of the hospital and what-have-you. You know, God, it looks like we're gonna lose the farm. Sure would be nice if somebody in the family could buy it—you know, for sentimental reasons."

When these "relatives" call they also feel obliged to give my number to somebody else. So when I've finally got that rare two hours at home with my kids, I end up spending thirty fascinating minutes on the phone with Wayne Hutton.

"Hey! I'm a distant cousin of your Uncle Mike. We's wunderin', if we come out to California, we talkin' about stoppin' by and see y'all a little bit. You know, just throw the kids out in the yard, shoot the shit for a while."

"Who are you?"

"Well, we love ya whole family. We've always been crazy about yer mama."

"But who are you?"

"Wayne Hutton, boy! Didn' I tell you?"

Afterward I called my mother. She said, "Seems to me like there *was* a cousin Wayne . . ."

These people show up at my concerts, too. They call my manager's office and say, "Hey, when Jeff comes to Missouri, tell him he's got some kinfolks out here and we'd like for him to come to dinner, if that'd be aright. He can just come out. Hell, you can come too if you want. By the way, we's wondering if we might get a few tickets fer the show.''

''Well, how many do you need?''

''Oh, 'bout forty-five'll do it.''

Afterward, they get mad if I won't come to the house. Frankly, I'm kind of scared to leave with them. Scared I may not come back.

Atlanta, being my hometown, is the most fun place for me to play. It's also the most aggravating. Every time I swear I will never do it again. Everybody with whom I went to elementary school, high school, and college wants to come to the show. Everybody I hung out with while I was single, worked with at IBM, ever dated (and now their husbands and kids), and every schoolteacher I had—all want to come to the show, God bless them. I get twenty complimentary tickets a night, I end up buying another hundred and fifty, and there are *still* always fifty people pissed off at me. Maybe what I'll do is this: JEFF FOXWORTHY, ONE NIGHT ONLY. THE PEOPLE-I-KNOW SHOW. Then they can feed me material from their seats. ''Hey, tell 'em about the time . . .''

When my first book, *You Might Be a Redneck If . . .* , came out, I finally had an inkling that my fortunes were improving. My family stopped telling me that I might eventually have to go back to my job at IBM. The lines at the malls were often as long for my book-signings as they were for the House of Venison ''young buck'' specials. I remember my mother telling me that she had the book at the family Christmas party. She said she stood in the middle of the room, reading the one-liners out loud, and everyone laughed. But on every third joke, all of a sudden, somebody wouldn't laugh—because they'd realized that the joke was about them.

''I started to read that one about 'if your junior-senior prom had a day care center . . .' " my mother said, "and all I could think about was your cousin Tracy sitting over there in the corner, and how she and Bob got married cause she got pregnant in the tenth grade."

I finally had to tell her, "Where do you think I come up with this stuff, Mom?"

Fans have heard me talk about my wife forever. Sometimes when we're out together, they'd rather talk to Gregg than to me.

Often when I play someplace and we know people in town, they'll invite Gregg to sit with them in the audience. She won't do that anymore. She says people end up not laughing every time I say something about her. That's because they turn to see how she's going to react.

You know, folks, it's not like she hasn't heard these jokes before. Almost every one of them began with me asking for her reaction. Our entire life is me coming out of the shower going, "Is this funny?"

It just hurts when she says yes before I've even told the joke. (Don't you make believe you don't know exactly what I mean.)

Being well known hasn't really affected my kids yet. They don't give a damn that I'm famous. I could have dinner at the White House, and that's not going to stop them from getting up seven times during the middle of the night. I'm just dad.

I've never really tried to explain my job to my daughters. One reason is that they're only two and four. But I think my oldest understands. The last time we went to see my wife's folks, we were walking through the New Orleans airport and she was riding on my shoulders. Somebody came up and wanted an autograph. I stopped—she's still on my shoulders—and I signed this thing. The guy said, "Thank you," and shook my hand, and walked off. She said, "Daddy, why do people like you so much?" I said, "I don't know, Peanut Butter, why do you think?" She said, "Cause you make them laugh." I turned to Gregg and said, "Wow."

All entertainers must wear makeup. This is important, especially if you're a man. For the first time in your life you've got something on your face all the time, besides a dumbass grin. But what happens if you leave the set or stage and you forget about it? There are you and your wife standing in the movie line, and all of a sudden it dawns on you: "Oh gosh, I'm still wearing mascara!"

One of the first times I ever wore makeup was when I did *Nashville Now* on TNN. I lived in Atlanta and I had to drive up to Tennessee to do the show, and then I had to drive back the same night to catch a plane in the morning for a gig somewhere else. Back then they put on *heavy* makeup. I'm talking the pancake stuff and the thick eyeliner.

I left right after the show and drove back to Atlanta through the north Georgia mountains. Suddenly red lights flashed and I saw a UFO—no, I got pulled over by the cops. I didn't think anything about it because I was only going about five miles an hour over the speed limit. Then the state trooper came up to the driver's window and he shined the light in my face. I could see right away that he felt *mean*. He looked like he'd been cast in *Smokey and the Bandit* and had been pissed ever since the production left town. I just sat there thinking, "Now, what have I done?"

When he finally spoke, my fears were realized. He said, "You gonna git yer ass outta the car, boy?" I did as he said. Meanwhile, he wouldn't take the flashlight off my face. I smiled and said, "Well, sir, what was I doing? I realize I was doing like sixty, okay, but I gotta get back to Atlanta and catch a flight tomorrow early, and . . . God, I'm *so* sorry . . ."

"Git yer ass back here to the back!" he said, walking toward the rear of my car. I followed, and then it hit me: "Shit, I've got

makeup on, in the middle of the night, in the north Georgia mountains, and a cop just pulled me over.'' There was only one thing I
could do. I stared him straight in the eye and said, ''You're looking
at the makeup, aren't cha?''

His lip curled and he said, ''Ye-ah.''

I said, ''Lemme explain. I *can* explain.''

''Ye-ah?''

''I was just on *Nashville Now,* and I left right from the set and
got in the car and started driving. I forgot to take off the makeup.''

He didn't say anything.

''It's the God's honest truth.''

Then he said, ''You on *Nashville Now*? All right, who's on there
tonight?''

''Porter Waggoner.''

''You *met* Porter Waggoner!''

''Yessir, I sure did.''

''What was he like?''

''Oh, he was as good as gold. Sir.''

''Aright, you kin go.''

This was a rare example of how *knowing* a celebrity can save
your butt. That and telling the truth. Otherwise, I might have ended
up as some skeleton that hunters find in the middle of deer season;
a collection of bones after the squirrels have already taken the
skull away.

You really know you're a celebrity when manufacturers send you
free stuff. You only get this after you reach the point where you
can finally afford it on your own. Travis Tritt and I were talking
about this on the set of my TV show one day.

He said, ''Tony Llama just gave me these boots.''

I said, ''Justin gave me *these* boots. Hell, you should see what
I've got piled up in my trailer.''

Then we both smiled and looked at each other. We knew what

the other guy was thinking: "Where were these people all those years when we couldn't afford anything?"

What really astounds me about being well known is how my life compares to my circumstances when I was growing up. In October 1995 I was able to charter a Learjet to take me to Atlanta to see the Braves play in the World Series. As we landed the Learjet, which cost a load of money, and taxied down the runway, we passed by the place where I lived, in Hapeville, at the end of the old airport runway. I looked out the window and thought, "That's where my house was. That house had one bathroom. It had a dirt yard. We burned trash in a barrel. Now I'm roaring past it in a Learjet I just rented to go see one stupid-ass ball game." So I asked myself, "How did I get from *there* to *here*?"

That's a good question.

I hope in some ways I've answered it.